MARY, QUEEN OF SCOTS
BOOK OF DAYS

This book belongs to:

_____

_____

_____

TUDOR ✖ TIMES

THE ORIGIN OF BOOKS OF HOURS

During the late Middle Ages and Renaissance period, one of the most coveted items a literate person could own was a Book of Hours.

They were designed to aid lay people in the practice of their religion by collecting biblical texts, prayers, and elements of the liturgy for them to read throughout the day, emulating the 'Hours' or regular services of the religious life.

By the late fifteenth century, Books of Hours were so popular that centres such as Paris and Bruges produced them en masse. Higher up the social scale, Books of Hours were individually commissioned, frequently as a bride-gift from husband to wife, and the level of decoration, the number of colours used in the illumination, and the quantity of gold, silver or expensive lapis blue used, depended on what the purchaser could afford. The Books were often personalised by the depiction of the owner's coat-of-arms or illustrations, such as the portraits adorning the Book of Hours of Anne of Brittany, Queen of France.

The Books were further individualised by the owner entering dates, such as the recording in 1489 by Lady Margaret Beaufort of the birth of Mary, Queen of Scots' grandmother. Often, friends or lovers would write verses to each other, an example being a loving exchange between King Henry VIII and Anne Boleyn.

Mary, Queen of Scots' Books of Hours

Mary herself had at least two Books of Hours. The first, the smallest known illuminated Book of Hours, measures only 2.9 x 2.3 inches. It has sixteen lines to a page, and was of Flemish provenance. Mary has written in it twice – one entry reading 'Mon dieu, confondez mes ennemys' (My God, confound my enemies). The limited illuminations suggest this was an everyday book, carried and referred to frequently.

Mary's second Book of Hours is housed in the National Library of Russia. It was made in France, probably in Paris, in the late 15th century, in the style of the Bedford Hours. Its original patron is unknown, although one theory is that it was made for the House of Luxembourg, so came to Mary via her grandmother, Anoinette de Bourbon. It consists of 229 parchment leaves, each decorated with an ornamental floral frame in colours and gold and containing 300 illuminated initial letters. The book has 22 miniatures which depict traditional subjects including the Annunciation, the Visitation of Mary to Elizabeth, the Nativity, the Adoration of the Magi and the Presentation at the Temple. The first three are pictures of the evangelists Luke, Matthew, and Mark. It also contains several entries by Mary herself, all in French. The first is a mark of ownership, 'Ce livre est à moi. Marie Reyne. 1554' which may suggest she received it to mark her sixteenth birthday. Mary treasured the book and took it with her into England, recording some of her most heartfelt sorrows in it. 'Qui jamais davantage eust contraire le sort, Si la vie m'est moins utile que la mort (to whom has the fate ever been more hostile, if my life is less useful for me than death).

As well as Mary's early signature, there is a second, dated 1579, and she also collected the signatures of others, including those of her father-in-law, the Earl of Lennox; Bess of Hardwick, wife of her gaoler, the Earl of Shrewsbury; the Earl of Leicester, Elizabeth I's favourite, and her niece-by-marriage, Lady Arbella Stuart.

When Mary was taken suddenly to Fotheringhay Castle in July 1586, an inventory of her possessions at Chartley was taken, and one Book of Hours is listed therein, suggesting that the other was on her person, probably the smaller, plainer book, which may the one she carried, along with a crucifix, to the scaffold.

MARY, QUEEN OF SCOTS BOOK OF DAYS

We cannot, alas, reproduce the extraordinary beauty of Mary's original Book of Hours but in the *Mary, Queen of Scots Book of Days*, we have sought to combine some of the functions of the originals in an attractive contemporary format. Our Book of Days is a perpetual calendar, which allows you to enter the events most important to you, your friends and family, and preserve them indefinitely, untrammelled by the days of the week or the year.

Mary never sought to undermine the Protestant religion that Scotland had adopted during her minority, but she remained firm in her own Catholic faith, and continued to observe the feast and saints' days of the traditional liturgical calendar, so these days are highlighted in every month. For each day of the year, there is an an event related to Mary or her family, friends or enemies. Each individual mentioned, or event that is not self-explanatory, has a short entry in the index. As well as a short overview of Mary's life, each month has a section on a specific event, and a description of a place that was important to the queen.

Notes

All dates are New Style – that is, the year begins on 1st January. Unless otherwise stated, the quotes for each month are by Mary. Church is used to refer to the Catholic Church, and Kirk to the Protestant. Although Mary's second husband, Henry Stuart, Lord Darnley, was known after their marriage as Henry, King of Scots, the name 'Darnley' is retained for clarity. Similarly, her third husband, James Hepburn, Earl of Bothwell was created Duke of Orkney, but remains Bothwell herein.

Messieurs ray honte destre contreinte
devons representer si particulierement
mes miseres pardeca mays le mal mepresse
s contreint de le vous declarer, a ce que
bon ne vous contento par de la de parolles
seus masleger par agun effect dont ze
suis hors de tonte osperance y ms gnezeue
voys rien a ceste feys que tande a parformar
cest honorable traittement dont il a tant reste
parle suir amyas maurt za signifie le responce
a mon memoire et depnis vne heure zay reeu
voz dermeres et hui et lautre lonsidere en
e ffect ze ne trenne ancqune occasion de
par vne voye ni lautre qui me fayt plus ryftement
q ne zauays vozprnze de pourszeuzure le conteun dema
leltrez zdes ubs

Vostre entierement meilleure amye
marie

A letter from Mary, Queen of Scots - she signs herself 'Marie'.

'IN MY END IS MY BEGINNING'
MARY, QUEEN OF SCOTS

THE LIFE OF MARY, QUEEN OF SCOTS

Mary was born at Linlithgow Palace on 8th December 1542. Within days, her father James V, defeated by the English at the Battle of Solway Moss, died, distraught at leaving the crown of Scotland to a girl, crying 'it cam wi' a lass, and it'll gang wi' a lass'. His fears were not unfounded – Henry VIII tried to follow up his army's victory by enforcing a marriage between Mary and his son Edward.

The Scots Parliament preferred the traditional Franco-Scottish alliance and, in 1548, Mary was secretly taken to France to marry François, heir to the French throne. There she received the education of a Renaissance princess, studying Latin, Italian, Spanish and the courtly arts – an upbringing intended to fit her for her role as Queen-Consort of France, rather than Queen of Scots. It was envisaged that her own country would be ruled for her by French regents, such as Mary's mother, Marie of Guise, who followed an initially popular pro-French, pro-Catholic strategy. Over time, this became harder as many of the Scots lords, including Mary's illegitimate half-brother, Lord James Stewart, committed themselves to the Protestant Reformation after encountering the charismatic preacher, John Knox. The newly Protestant nobles formed themselves in 1557 into the Lords of the Congregation, determined to reform Scotland's religion.

Mary married François on 24th April 1558 and the couple were encouraged to claim the crown of England on the death of Mary I of England, as, in Catholic eyes, the new English queen, Elizabeth I, was illegitimate. Elizabeth was pursuing a Protestant policy, giving the Lords of the Congregation an alternative to French domination.

François succeeded to the French throne in 1559, but his reign was all too brief. He died in December 1560, and it was soon clear that Mary was no longer welcome in France. It was an opportune time for her to return to Scotland. Marie of Guise had died in June 1560, and the government was in the hands of Lord James, who had negotiated the Treaty of Edinburgh, acknowledging Elizabeth as Queen of England and agreeing the withdrawal of French troops from Scotland. Mary refused to ratify the treaty, but she agreed with Lord James that she would return, on the understanding that the legislation of 1560 that had made Scotland a Protestant country would remain, whilst she would continue, privately, in her Catholic faith.

Aged eighteen, Mary was confronted with ruling a country that was poor, factious, religiously divided, and with a neighbour in Elizabeth who entertained the deepest suspicions of Mary's motives. Mary's upbringing in France, a highly centralised and authoritarian monarchy, had ill-prepared her for the realities of the Scottish situation. Nevertheless, her personal rule began promisingly. Her subjects were delighted with her youth and beauty, and, not being a woman of dogmatic or over-bearing character, she was willing to learn from Lord James and other senior statesmen – although she would not be their puppet.

Mary planned to marry, to secure an heir. The difficulty was that, in a male-dominated world, her husband would become king of Scots. Her initial choice of Don Carlos, son of Philip II of Spain, was refused. Elizabeth offered her the hand of her own favourite, Robert Dudley, Earl of Leicester, an offensive suggestion that angered Mary. In any event, her thoughts had turned elsewhere.

Henry Stuart, Lord Darnley, was, like Mary, a great-grandchild of Henry VII, giving him a claim to the English throne which would strengthen Mary's own position. In addition, Darnley was the right age, handsome, charming and accomplished. It seemed a match made in heaven. Mary was enchanted and married him on 29th July 1565.

Lord James, now Earl of Moray, was not pleased by this Catholic newcomer ousting him from his role as the queen's right-hand man. He and other senior Protestant Lords rebelled and attempted to take Edinburgh. Mary speedily gathered her forces and, in what became known as the Chaseabout Raid, drove Moray into England. Mary increased her number of advisers, bringing both Catholics and Protestants into her Council.

Good on paper, Mary's marriage proved disastrous. Darnley was spoilt, drunken and probably syphilitic. He dreamed of power, without the ability to use it effectively and Mary quickly repented her marriage. Darnley, rather than supporting his wife, demanded the Crown Matrimonial – this would not only have made him king of Scots in fact, as well as in name, but would have allowed him to continue as monarch during his lifetime, even if Mary pre-deceased him. Mary robustly refused. He raged and sulked, and, eventually, conspired with the rebellious Protestant Lords to capture Mary. Darnley and his men burst into Mary's apartments at Holyrood Palace, dragged her secretary, David Riccio, screaming out of the room and stabbed him to death. Mary was restrained by her husband, whilst a loaded pistol was pointed at her heavily-pregnant belly. The following twenty-four hours showed Mary at her best. Locked into her apartments with Darnley, she persuaded him that his co-conspirators would turn their attentions to him next and they hatched an escape plan. A message was smuggled out to her supporters to have horses brought, and she and Darnley slipped out of the palace and fled into the night. Before long, Mary was back in control. On 19th June 1566 she gave birth to a healthy son.

Darnley continued to be a liability. Mary contemplated annulment, but that would have affected the prince's legitimacy. Moray and the other lords were equally tired of him. No-one knows for certain who was responsible, but one reasonable inference is there was a plot hatched by others to dispose of Darnley and that Mary preferred not to know about it. Mary effected a reconciliation with Darnley and encouraged him to return to Edinburgh, where she nursed him through a bout of illness. One evening she left his sickbed for a wedding party. That night, his house blew up. His body was found in the garden, with no evidence of the explosion – he had been suffocated.

The politic course of action for Mary to take, whether innocent or guilty, was to express horror, dress in mourning, find some scapegoats and hang them. What actually happened was that she was seen frequently with the prime suspect, the Earl of Bothwell. No steps were taken to find out who had been responsible until, eventually, Darnley's father, the Earl of Lennox, brought a prosecution against Bothwell. Ignoring all advice, Mary made her support of Bothwell plain and he was acquitted.

In April 1567, Bothwell abducted Mary and probably raped her. Whoever had been responsible for the murder, the Lords now backed off from the queen who, instead of having Bothwell arrested and punished, married him, perhaps knowing herself pregnant. This was too much for the public and the Lords to bear. Mary and Bothwell's army faced that of the Lords on 15th June 1567 at Carberry Hill.

Unwilling to shed blood, Mary surrendered, believing she would be treated honourably, but she was paraded through the streets of Edinburgh, as murderess and whore, and imprisoned at Lochleven. On 24th July, a delegation intimidated Mary into abdicating in favour of her son who was proclaimed James VI. Resourceful as ever, Mary escaped and raised another army, but was defeated in the field at Langside. Then, she made her worst mistake. Instead of fleeing to France, she crossed the Solway Firth into England, believing her sister-queen, Elizabeth, would help her.

Mary's confidence proved to be misplaced and she was held in honourable confinement until she could prove her innocence of the murder of Darnley. A tribunal was held at York, but Mary refused to acknowledge its jurisdiction. She was a queen, and not a subject of England. The evidence presented (sent by Moray, now regent for James) consisted of the documents known as the Casket Letters which contained incriminating material purporting to be from Mary to Bothwell. Mary rejected them as forgeries – her writing was not hard to imitate. The documents were later destroyed, and the available copies have been interpreted variously as genuine, as forgeries or partially genuine with forged interpolations.

The tribunal came to no conclusion, the ideal outcome for Elizabeth, so for nineteen years Mary remained a prisoner. Although incarcerated, Mary still managed to involve herself in plots against Elizabeth. From her perspective, this was entirely justified. She was being held against her will and she had warned the English government that

'If I shall be holden here perforce, you may be sure then, being as a desperate person, I will use any attempts that may serve my purpose, either by myself or by my friends.'

Over the years, the Rising of the Northern Earls, the Ridolfi Plot, the Throckmorton Plot and finally, the Babington Plot, aimed to free Mary and to place her on the throne. The schemes were variously backed by France and Spain and, perhaps, in the case of the Babington Plot, fomented by the English government to entrap Mary. In the latter case, letters were smuggled in and out in beer barrels supplied by a brewer who was secretly in the pay of Sir Francis Walsingham, Elizabeth's Secretary of State. Finally, Mary responded to a letter in which a plan for Elizabeth's assassination was explicitly stated. She did not demur at such a step, and this was enough for Elizabeth to agree to a trial. Mary was tried at Fotheringhay Castle by thirty-eight nobles, of whom only one dissented at her conviction for treason, although Mary reiterated that, as she was not a subject of England, she could not be guilty.

Elizabeth was reluctant to sign the death warrant – if an anointed monarch could be executed, that would undermine sovereigns everywhere. But England was in a defensive state: it was known that Philip II of Spain was planning an invasion – it was imperative that there be no Catholic heir whom he could use to replace Elizabeth. Eventually, she signed the warrant and Mary was executed on 8th February, 1587. Initially laid to rest at Peterborough Cathedral, in 1612 her son, James VI, now James I of England, had her reinterred in Westminster Abbey.

'SOME OF OUR SUBJECTS AND
COUNCIL BY THEIR PROCEEDINGS
HAVE DECLARED MANIFESTLY WHAT
MEN THEY ARE... SLAIN OUR MOST
SPECIAL SERVANT IN OUR OWN
PRESENCE AND THEREAFTER HELD
OUR PROPER PERSON CAPTIVE
TREASONABLY.'

MARY, QUEEN OF SCOTS

ELEGY

The art of poetry was an important courtly accomplishment. Mary was tutored by the French court poet, Ronsard. She wrote a long elegy after the death of her first husband, and this poignant poem during her incarceration at Fotheringhay

Que suis-je hélas? Et de quoi sert ma vie?
Je ne suis fors qu'un corps privé de coeur,
Une ombre vaine, un objet de malheur
Qui n'a plus rien que de mourir en vie.

Plus ne me portez, O ennemis, d'envie
A qui n'a plus l'esprit à la grandeur.
J'ai consommé d'excessive douleur
Votre ire en bref de voir assouvie.

Et vous, amis, qui m'avez tenue chère,
Souvenez-vous que sans coeur et sans santé
Je ne saurais aucune bonne oeuvre faire,
Souhaitez donc fin de calamité

Et que, ici-bas étant assez punie,
J'aie ma part en la joie infinie.

FACTS ABOUT
MARY, QUEEN OF SCOTS

1. Although Mary was brought up at the French court, she continued to speak Scots, similar to, but not, English. She learnt English only when incarcerated in England.

2. Mary had four close friends who accompanied her to France – they all had the same Christian name and were known as the Four Marys – Beaton, Seton, Fleming and Livingstone.

3. After she had been in France for three years, her mother, Marie of Guise visited her. Mary was unable to maintain the dignified pose expected of her during the formal reception and ran into her mother's arms.

4. Since Mary was a sovereign queen, she was not crowned as queen-consort of France.

5. Mary led her own army against the rebellious Earl of Huntly, dressed in armour with pistols at her side.

6. Mary continued the tradition of Scottish kings by hearing legal cases in person.

7. Mary and her ladies horrified John Knox by dressing in breeches for sport.

8. Mary may have played an early form of billiards.

9. Mary worked with her nemesis, John Knox, to reconcile the marital difficulties of her half-sister, Jean and Jean's husband, the Earl of Argyll.

10. When imprisoned at Lochleven, Mary miscarried twins, fathered by her third husband, the Earl of Bothwell.

11. Mary's second mother-in-law, Margaret, Countess of Lennox, sent Mary a handkerchief embroidered using the countess's own hair.

12. Mary's last letter was to her brother-in-law, Henri III of France.

13. Mary's last message to her friends was that she 'died a true woman of her religion and a like a true Scottish woman and a true French woman.'

PERSONAL DETAILS

Name

Surname

Home address

Telephone

Mobile

Email

Date of birth

Place of birth

Website

Wi-Fi

Login

Home Wi-Fi

Login

Family doctor	Dentist
Address	Address
Telephone	Telephone
Blood group	
Allergies	
Vaccinations	
Passport No	
Valid until	
Visa	
Expiry date	
Driving licence	
Expiry date	

Year planner

January	February	March

April	May	June

July

August

September

October

November

December

MONTH PLANNER

January

1   Mary granted her own household, having been declared of age a year early (1554)

2   Mary arrived at Tutbury Castle in Staffordshire (1570)

3   Embassy from Lords of the Congregation to Elizabeth I returned to Edinburgh (1560)

4   Final day of Mary's four-day stay at Seton Palace in East Lothian (1562)

5   Catherine de' Medici, Mary's mother-in-law, died (1589)

6   Mary attended wedding of her friend, Mary Fleming, to Sir William Maitland (1567)

7   The body of James V was taken from Falkland Palace to Edinburgh (1543)

8   Funeral of James V at Holyrood Abbey (1543)

9   Earl of Morton returned to Scotland from exile in England (1566)

10   The Reformation Parliament opened (1560)

11   Elizabeth I closed Westminster Conference with no definitive verdict (1569)

12   Mary pleaded with Elizabeth I to end suspense of her death sentence (1587)

13   Mary stayed at Stirling Castle (1563)

14   Mary moved herself and her son, James, to Holyroodhouse (1567)

15   Elizabeth I was crowned Queen of England (1559)

16   Duke of Norfolk found guilty of treason for planning to marry Mary (1572)

17   Mary stayed at Linlithgow Palace in West Lothian (1562)

18   Spanish ambassador, de Silva, reported Mary had rejected plot to assassinate Darnley (1567)

19   François II, King of France, Mary's first husband, was born (1544)

20   Mary set out for Glasgow, where a sick Lord Darnley was staying with his father (1567)

21   Mary was deprived of her personal servants (1587)

22   Antoinette de Bourbon, Duchess of Guise, Mary's grandmother, died (1583)

23   Earl of Moray, regent for James VI, assassinated (1570)

24   James, Earl of Bothwell, captured and imprisoned by the English (1563)

25   Mary stayed at Linlithgow Palace (1562)

26   Mary was moved from Bolton Castle, following a six-month stay (1569)

27   Mary and Lord Darnley left Glasgow to return to Edinburgh (1567)

28   Henry VIII of England died (1547)

29   Mary stayed at St Andrews in Fife (1565)

30   Mary secretly granted earldom of Moray to Lord James Stewart (1562)

31   Mary promised Pius V she would restore Catholicism to Scotland and England (1566)

Birthdays	Anniversaries	Reminders	Projects

Gardening	Events	Occasions	Festivals

RECONCILIATION WITH DARNLEY

Mary married her cousin, Lord Darnley, despite considerable opposition. The match was excellent in theory – Darnley, like Mary, was a descendant of Henry VII of England, which would enhance their children's claim to the English Crown. He was of similar age to the queen, well-educated, tall, handsome, charming, and nominally Catholic. What was hidden from Mary during their courtship, was Darnley's weak, spoilt and arrogant character.

Immediately after the wedding on 29th July 1565 Mary had Darnley proclaimed king but it was soon apparent that misgivings over his character were justified. Although he performed his primary task, with Mary soon falling pregnant, he demanded more money than she could afford, and also that she petition Parliament for him to be granted the Crown Matrimonial.

A plot was laid by malcontent nobles to inveigle Darnley into a scheme which, he was told, would give him the Crown Matrimonial. One night, whilst Mary was having supper with friends and her secretary, Riccio, of whom Darnley was irrationally jealous, Darnley and Lord Ruthven burst in leading a band of armed men. Mary was seized by her husband, and one of the conspirators pointed a pistol at her pregnant belly.

Riccio was stabbed to death.

Undaunted by being in the power of her enemies, Mary pinpointed her husband as the weak link in their plans, and she persuaded him that his life, as well as hers, was in danger. Lulling the rebels into carelessness by claiming her labour had begun, she and Darnley slipped out of the palace and galloped to Dunbar Castle. Within two weeks Mary was back in Edinburgh, apparently safe on her throne, with the rebels scattered. She tried to put a good face on her marriage – no annulment was possible lest it damage the legitimacy of her child, James, born in June 1566.

Mary and her councillors discussed the problem of Darnley at Craigmillar Castle on 20th November 1566. Mary insisted that her honour must not be compromised and was assured that her councillors would do nothing but what was 'good and approved by Parliament'.

In January 1567, Mary and Darnley were apparently reconciled. He returned to Edinburgh staying in a house at Kirk o'Field where, on 10th February, Mary visited him before attending a wedding party at Holyrood. Later that night an explosion rocked the house to its foundations, and Darnley was found dead in the garden, probably suffocated.

CHATEAU D'AMBOISE

Mary spent most of her childhood in France at the Chateau d'Amboise, where she was brought up with the children of Henri II and Catherine de' Medici.

The French court was based in the Loire Valley for much of the fifteenth and sixteenth centuries, and at Chateau d'Amboise for most of that period. Originally a twelfth-century fortress, it was seized from Louis d'Amboise by Charles VII in 1434, and substantially extended and rebuilt into a luxurious palace by Charles VIII at the end of that century. Located on a plateau, high above the river, the magnificent palace dominated the skyline, highly visible for miles around.

François I embellished and enhanced the palace using the latest Italian designs and his glittering Renaissance court attracted artists and literary figures from across Europe. Leonardo da Vinci, who lived at nearby Clos Lucé, was a frequent visitor towards the end of his life and was buried there in the Collegiate Church of St Florentin. His tomb, now in the St Hubert Chapel within the palace grounds, can still be visited today.

It was to this Renaissance palace, with its spectacular interiors and formal gardens, that Mary came as a young child and lived during her formative years in France. Her father-in-law,

Henri II, had a new wing constructed with apartments especially fitted out for his children and Mary.

A much darker note is the palace's role in the Amboise Conspiracy. In 1560, a Huguenot plot to capture François II and Mary and free them from the influence of Mary's Guise relatives was foiled. On its discovery, the couple fled from Blois to the comparative safety of Amboise. However, there ensued a bloody massacre with grim reprisals. Nobles were decapitated on the terrace at Amboise and the corpses of hundreds of lesser men were hung from the balcony over the Loire.

Following these traumatic events, François II's younger brothers, later Charles IX and Henri III, used Amboise much less than their predecessors. It gradually fell into decline, used as a prison in the seventeenth century and partially demolished after the French Revolution. Occupation by the German army and Allied bombing during World War II also took their toll. However, following a substantial restoration campaign, much of the palace built by Charles VIII remains today and has been restored to former glories.

It is owned by the Saint-Louis Foundation and is open to visitors throughout the year.

JANUARY

1   **Feast of the Circumcision**

Mary granted her own
household after being
declared of age a year early
(1554)

2   **St Basil the Great's Day**

Mary arrived at Tutbury
Castle in Staffordshire
(1570)

3   **St Genevieve of Paris' Day**

Embassy from Lords of the
Congregation to Elizabeth I
returned to Edinburgh
(1560)

4 **Octave of the Holy Innocents**

Final day of Mary's four-day stay at Seton Palace in East Lothian (1562)

5 **Vigil of the Epiphany**

Catherine de' Medici, Mary's mother-in-law, died (1589)

6 **Feast of the Epiphany**

Mary attended wedding of her friend, Mary Fleming, to Sir William Maitland (1567)

7   **St Cedd, Bishop of London's, Day**

The body of James V was taken from Falkland Palace to Edinburgh (1543)

8   **St Wulsin's Day**

Funeral of James V at Holyrood Abbey (1543)

9   Earl of Morton returned to Scotland from exile in England (1566)

10 **St Geraint of Wales' Day**

The Reformation
Parliament opened (1560)

11 **St Brandan's Day**

Elizabeth I closed the
Westminster Conference
with no definitive verdict
(1569)

12 Mary pleaded with
Elizabeth I to end suspense
of her death sentence (1587)

JANUARY

13 **St Mungo of Scotland's Day**

Mary stayed at Stirling Castle (1563)

14 **St Felix of Nola's Day**

Mary moved herself and her son, James, to Holyroodhouse (1567)

15 **St Isidore's Day**

Elizabeth I was crowned Queen of England (1559)

16 St Marcellus' Day

Duke of Norfolk found
guilty of treason for
planning to marry Mary
(1572)

17 St Antony of Egypt's Day

Mary stayed at Linlithgow
Palace in West Lothian
(1562)

18 St Prisca's Day

Spanish ambassador, de
Silva, reported Mary had
rejected plot to assassinate
Darnley (1567)

JANUARY

19 St Wulstan's Day

François II, King of France,
Mary's first husband, was
born (1544)

20 SS Fabian and Sebastian's
Day

Mary set out for Glasgow,
where a sick Lord Darnley
was staying with his father
(1567)

21 St Agnes

Mary was deprived of her
personal servants (1587)

22 **St Anastasius' Day**

Antoinette de Bourbon,
Duchess of Guise, Mary's
grandmother, died (1583)

23 Earl of Moray, regent for
James VI, assassinated
(1570)

24 **St Timothy**

James, Earl of Bothwell,
captured and imprisoned by
the English (1563)

JANUARY

25 **Feast of the Conversion of Paul**

Mary stayed at Linlithgow Palace (1562)

26 **St Polycarp's Day**

Mary was moved from Bolton Castle, following a six-month stay (1569)

27 **St John Chrysostom's Day**

Mary and Lord Darnley left Glasgow to return to Edinburgh (1567)

28 **Octave of St Agnes**

Henry VIII of England
died (1547)

_____

29 **St Valerius' Day**

Mary stayed at St Andrews
in Fife (1565)

_____

30 **St Adelgundis' Day**

Mary secretly granted
earldom of Moray to Lord
James Stewart (1562)

JANUARY

31 Mary promised Pius V she would restore Catholicism to Scotland and England (1566)

Notes

Notes

MONTH PLANNER

February

1 Elizabeth I signed Mary's death warrant (1587)

2 Lord Darnley was invested with the Order of St Michel (1566)

3 English Privy Council signed commission to issue Mary's death warrant (1587)

4 Mary arrived at Tutbury Castle, Staffordshire, for the first time (1569)

5 Mary spent night at Kirk o'Field after helping Lord Darnley take a medicinal bath (1567)

6 Mary stayed at Holyroodhouse (1562)

7 Earls of Kent and Shrewsbury delivered her execution warrant to Mary (1587)

8 Mary was executed in the Great Hall at Fotheringhay Castle (1587)

9 Sir William Maitland wrote to Sir William Cecil, hinting at murder of Riccio (1565)

10 Henry, Lord Darnley, King of Scots, assassinated in Edinburgh (1567)

11 Henry, Lord Darnley, arrived in Scotland (1565)

12 Mary stayed at Lundie Castle (1565)

13 English ambassador informed Earl of Leicester of plot to murder Riccio (1566)

14 Funeral in Edinburgh of Earl of Moray, Regent of Scotland (1570)

15 Mary stayed at Falkland Palace (1563)

16 Placard placed on Tolbooth, accusing Bothwell of Darnley's murder (1567)

17 Henry, Lord Darnley, met Mary at Wemyss Castle in Fife (1564)

18 Mary stayed at St Andrews in Fife (1563)

19 Duke of Châtelherault relinquished governorship to Mary's mother, Marie of Guise (1554)

20 Edward VI was crowned King of England & Ireland (1547)

21 Countess of Lennox, Mary's mother-in-law, released from Tower of London to house arrest (1567)

22 Marie of Guise was crowned Queen-consort of Scots at Holyrood Abbey (1540)

23 Pacification of Perth, ending civil war in Scotland (1573)

24 Elizabeth I advised Mary on how to handle crisis of Darnley's murder (1567)

25 Randolph wrote full account of plot in hand to murder Riccio (1566)

26 Mary stayed at St Andrews (1563)

27 Treaty of Berwick signed by Lords of the Congregation and Elizabeth I (1560)

28 Mary proclaimed Duke of Châtelherault her lieutenant in Scotland (1569)

29 Lords Livingston and Erskine took Mary to Dumbarton en route for France (1548)

Birthdays	Anniversaries	Reminders	Projects

Gardening	Events	Occasions	Festivals

MARY'S EXECUTION

In September 1586, in the wake of the Babington Plot, Mary was conveyed to Fotheringhay Castle in Northamptonshire. Thirty-six commissioners were summoned to try her under the Act of Association – which provided that anyone who might benefit from a plot to assassinate Elizabeth I would be considered guilty of treason. The French ambassador requested Elizabeth to allow Mary counsel for her defence but was brusquely rejected. The trial had no basis in law – Mary was not a subject of the English queen, and thus, as she frequently repeated, not subject to English law. Elizabeth was aware of this, and of the risks inherent in permitting a sovereign to be tried at all. Nevertheless, the threat of Spanish invasion and Catholic resurgence was so feared that she permitted the trial to proceed.

The commission did not pass sentence. Instead, it was left to Parliament to pronounce that, the case having been proven against Mary, she must be sentenced to death. Elizabeth hesitated over signing the death warrant until early February, when it was taken to Fotheringhay, alongside instructions to the earls of Shrewsbury and Kent on how the execution was to be conducted. On the evening of 7th February 1587, Shrewsbury read the warrant and informed Mary that she would die the following morning. She was refused the comfort of a Catholic priest and her request to be buried alongside her mother or her first husband in France. She wrote her will and a last letter to her brother-in-law, Henri III of France, requesting that he succour her servants.

Early the next day the earls escorted Mary, dressed in black and carrying her ivory crucifix and a book of hours, to the Great Hall. She mounted the hastily-erected scaffold, then, removing her gown, revealed a kirtle of blood-red, the colour of martyrdom. Before kneeling to receive the blow from the axe, she sent a last message to her friends that she 'died a true woman of her religion and like a true Scottish woman and a true French woman'.

Mary's remains were wrapped in lead and left at Fotheringhay until July when she was interred in a Protestant ceremony at Peterborough Cathedral, under the royal banner of the Scottish lion. The Countess of Bedford was chief mourner.

Mary's son, James VI & I, later had her reinterred in Westminster Abbey, spending double the amount on her tomb that he spent on Elizabeth's.

FOTHERINGHAY CASTLE

Fotheringhay Castle, a twelfth-century castle located in the English midlands, was to become Mary's final prison and the site of her trial and subsequent execution.

The castle, originally a Norman stronghold of motte and bailey design, came into royal hands when seized by Edward I in the late thirteenth century. By the fifteenth century it had been transformed into a substantial seat of power and luxurious residence for Richard, Duke of York, leading protagonist in the Wars of the Roses, and his wife, Cecily Neville. Their youngest child, Richard III, was born there in October 1452. The neighbouring Church of St Mary and All Saints also has strong Yorkist connections, and its mausoleum contains the tombs of Richard, Duke of York, Duchess Cecily, and their son Edmund, Earl of Rutland. All were ancestors of Mary through her paternal grandmother, Margaret Tudor, Queen-consort of Scotland.

Following Richard III's death at the Battle of Bosworth, Henry VII granted Fotheringhay to Elizabeth of York and it subsequently became part of the jointure of all Henry VIII's queens.

Mary was moved to Fotheringhay Castle from Chartley Manor in Staffordshire on 25th September 1586, following the discovery of the Babington Plot. Located in a marshy area, Fotheringhay is isolated and difficult to access, particularly in the winter. It was further south than the other places in which Mary had been held, away from potential Catholic support in the North, but still a considerable distance from London.

Mary's trial was held in the Great Hall at Fotheringhay on 14th-15th October 1586 and she was executed there on 8th February 1587. A large platform was built as a scaffold and some three hundred spectators were crammed in to witness the event. Following her death, Mary's clothes and prayer book and everything associated with the beheading were burnt to prevent the keeping of relics.

By 1592, the castle was being used for militia stores and it fell into disrepair from the 1620s, with locals removing much of the stone for building. All that remains now is the old motte, traces of the bailey and moat and a small fragment of masonry.

It is possible to visit the site and to walk where the privy lodgings and Great Hall of the castle once stood. The Church of St Mary and All Saints is also open to visitors.

FEBRUARY

1   Elizabeth I signed Mary's
death warrant (1587)

2   **Feast of the Purification of
the Virgin (Candlemas)**

Lord Darnley was invested
with the Order of St Michel
(1566)

3   **St Wereburghe**

English Privy Council
signed commission to issue
Mary's death warrant (1587)

4 **St Gilbert's Day**

Mary arrived at Tutbury Castle, Staffordshire, for the first time (1569)

5 **St Abraham of Arbela's Day**

Mary spent night at Kirk o' Field after helping Lord Darnley take a medicinal bath (1567)

6 **St Dorothy's Day**

Mary stayed at Holyroodhouse (1562)

FEBRUARY

7 Earls of Kent and
Shrewsbury delivered her
execution warrant to Mary
(1587)

8 Mary was executed in the
Great Hall at Fotheringhay
Castle (1587)

9 **St Apollonia's Day**

Sir William Maitland
wrote to Sir William Cecil,
hinting at murder of Riccio
(1565)

10 Henry, Lord Darnley, King
of Scots, assassinated in
Edinburgh (1567)

11 Henry, Lord Darnley,
arrived in Scotland (1565)

12 Mary stayed at Lundie
Castle (1565)

February

13 English ambassador
informed Earl of Leicester
of plot to murder Riccio
(1566)

14 St Valentine's Day

Funeral in Edinburgh of
Earl of Moray, Regent of
Scotland (1570)

15 SS Faustinus and Jovita's
Day

Mary stayed at Falkland
Palace (1563)

FEBRUARY

16 **St Juliana's Day**

Placard placed on Tolbooth, accusing Bothwell of Darnley's murder (1567)

17 **Feast of the Flight into Egypt**

Henry, Lord Darnley, met Mary at Wemyss Castle in Fife (1564)

18 **St Simon of Jerusalem's Day**

Mary stayed at St Andrews in Fife (1563)

43

FEBRUARY

19 Duke of Châtelherault
relinquished governorship
to Mary's mother, Marie of
Guise (1554)

20 Edward VI was crowned
King of England & Ireland
(1547)

21 Countess of Lennox, Mary's
mother-in-law, released
from Tower of London to
house arrest (1567)

22 Marie of Guise was
crowned Queen-consort of
Scots at Holyrood Abbey
(1540)

23 **St Oswald's Day**

Pacification of Perth,
ending civil war in Scotland
(1573)

24 **St Matthias' Day**

Elizabeth I advised Mary
on how to handle crisis of
Darnley's murder (1567)

FEBRUARY

25 Randolph wrote a full account of the plot in hand to murder Riccio (1566)

26 Mary stayed at St Andrews (1563)

27 **St Leander's Day**

Treaty of Berwick signed by Lords of the Congregation and Elizabeth I (1560)

28 SS Romanus and Lupicinus' Day

Mary proclaimed Duke of
Châtelherault her lieutenant
in Scotland (1569)

29 St Matthias Day

Lords Livingston and
Erskine took Mary to
Dumbarton en route for
France (1548)

Notes

February

Notes

Notes

MONTH PLANNER

March

1   Placards linking Mary and Bothwell in adultery and Darnley's murder circulated in Edinburgh (1567)

2   Moray signed conspirators' bond for assassination of Riccio (1566)

3   Elizabeth I wrote to Mary castigating her for her treatment of Moray (1566)

4   Mary stayed in Perth (1564)

5   Elizabeth I ended any prospect of Mary marrying Leicester and being named her heir (1565)

6   Mary's friend, Mary Livingston, married John Sempill (1565)

7   Mary went in state to open Parliament, flanked by earls of Huntly, Crawford and Bothwell (1565)

8   Darnley signed a passport permitting Moray to return to Scotland (1565)

9   Riccio was dragged from Mary's presence and murdered (1566)

10   Moray returned from being exiled after the Chaseabout Raid (1566)

11   Mary and Darnley escaped from Holyroodhouse to Dunbar Castle after Riccio's murder (1566)

12   Parliament appointed Earl of Arran as Governor and Tutor to Mary (1543)

13   Moray requested a passport to enter England from Sir William Cecil (1567)

14   John Knox, Protestant evangelist, invited by Scottish nobles to return to Scotland (1557)

15   Four Scottish nobles given joint physical custody of the young Mary (1543)

16   Marie of Guise's remains were shipped to France for burial (1561)

17   Mary issued a summons to loyal subjects to attend her, armed, at Dunbar (1566)

18   Mary re-entered Edinburgh at the head of her army (1566)

19   Mary sent Prince James under guard to Stirling Castle to protection of Earl of Mar (1567)

20   Darnley swore to Privy Council he had no part in planning Riccio's murder (1566)

21   Last day of Mary's two-week stay at St Andrews (1562)

22   Mary stayed at Falkland Palace (1562)

23   English Privy Council advised Elizabeth I that Mary and François II of France were her mortal enemies (1560)

24   Mary agreed to Lennox's demand that Bothwell stand trial for Darnley's murder (1567)

25   Marry arrived at Pitlethie House in Fife for a five-day stay (1563)

26   John Knox exiled from Frankfurt (1556)

27   James VI & I died at Theobalds in Hertfordshire, England (1625)

28   Mary secluded herself to pray for four hours on this Good Friday (1567)

29   Sixty-eight men were attainted for their part in the murder of Riccio (1566)

30   Mary responded to Elizabeth I's suggestion that she marry Leicester (1564)

31   Henri II of France was born (1519) and acceded to the throne (1547)

Birthdays	Anniversaries	Reminders	Projects

Gardening	Events	Occasions	Festivals

THE REBELLION OF MORAY

During her time in France, Mary's illegitimate half-brother, Lord James Stewart, converted to Protestantism, and became chief of the Lords of the Congregation. In June 1560, he took over the regency of Scotland and introduced legislation to make Scotland Protestant. In December 1560 Mary informed Lord James that she planned to return to Scotland. Despite warnings that Lord James coveted her throne, Mary accepted his suggestion that she return under the condition of recognising Protestantism as Scotland's religion, although she would maintain her Catholic faith.

For four years Lord James, promoted to the earldom of Moray, was by Mary's side, her seemingly devoted and trustworthy councillor. But when Mary chose to marry Darnley, against Moray's advice, he quickly showed another side of his character, withdrawing from court and requesting Elizabeth I to send £3,000 to support the Protestant faith – presumably through armed rebellion. After he refused a summons to the royal presence to explain himself, Mary outlawed him. His lands were declared forfeit and Mary mustered troops at Edinburgh. No sooner had she and her army marched out of Edinburgh than Moray entered with three allies, who were soon dismayed to discover they had no support.

Mary pursued Moray in what became known as the 'Chaseabout Raid' as royal and rebel armies marched hither and thither across the south of Scotland, never coming to blows. Moray requested help from England. Elizabeth would not openly support rebels, but offered £1,000 and sanctuary, which Moray accepted, settling in Newcastle. Soon, he and other disaffected nobles hatched a plan to inveigle Darnley into the murder of Mary's secretary, Riccio, to take control of Mary, and to force her to pardon Moray.

Mary opened Parliament requesting that an act of attainder be passed against Moray. The debate was scheduled for 12th March 1566, precipitating the rebels' action. That night, Riccio was murdered, whilst the pregnant queen was restrained. Within hours, Moray appeared. Mary did not seem to realise that he could only have arrived so promptly if he had been involved in the plot, and rushed into his arms, protesting that, had he been there, she would not have been so mistreated.

Mary escaped, taking an apparently penitent Darnley with her. Within two weeks she was back in Edinburgh, apparently safe on her throne, with the rebels scattered. Moray was back by her side – his part in the murder unknown to her.

PALACE OF HOLYROODHOUSE

Mary's official residence, it was the one she used most frequently during her personal rule and appears to have been her favourite, despite the terrible murder she witnessed there.

Located at the bottom of the Royal Mile, at the other end from Edinburgh Castle, the Palace of Holyroodhouse was built next to Holyrood Abbey by James IV for his new English bride, Margaret Tudor, in the first decade of the sixteenth century. In the previous century, Stewart monarchs had increasingly used lodgings at Holyrood Abbey, with its pleasant gardens and large orchards, when staying in Edinburgh, in preference to those of the cramped and windy castle.

James IV built a modern Renaissance palace, incorporating part of the Abbey's church and cloister into its quadrangular plan. James V undertook major works, modifying and extending his father's palace, and building the large, rectangular north-west tower that is so well recognised today. It is here that Mary had her privy apartments – a suite of three rooms, consisting of her bedchamber, supper room and outer chamber. It is here too that her private secretary, David Riccio, was stabbed to death in her presence by the Lords, who then briefly held Mary captive.

The palace caught fire in 1650 during a visit by Oliver Cromwell and his soldiers and it was rebuilt by Charles II in the 1670s. Luckily, the north-west tower is one of the few parts of the palace to survive from Mary's time. Her rooms remain, with their sixteenth-century wooden ceilings, wall panelling and painted friezes. It is possible, after climbing the narrow, steep staircase, to see these small, intimate rooms in which Mary lived and Riccio was murdered.

Holyroodhouse has other strong associations with Mary. She married both her Scottish husbands here; Lord Darnley in the chapel in 1565 and the Earl of Bothwell in the great hall in 1567. Her grandparents, James IV and Margaret Tudor, were married in the neighbouring abbey church; her mother, Marie of Guise, was crowned there and her father James V, was buried there; as was Lord Darnley and both her infant brothers.

Today, Holyroodhouse, the official residence of Her Majesty The Queen in Scotland, is managed by the Royal Collections Trust and open to the public throughout the year. So, too, are the ruins of the adjacent Holyrood Abbey, in the care of Historic Environment Scotland.

MARCH

1   St David's Day

Placards linking Mary and
Bothwell in adultery and
Darnley's murder circulated
in Edinburgh (1567)

2   St Aelred of Rievaulx' Day

Moray signed conspirators'
bond for assassination of
Riccio (1566)

3   St Cunigundus' Day

Elizabeth I wrote to Mary
castigating her for her
treatment of Moray (1566)

4 **St Casimir of Poland's Day**

Mary stayed in Perth (1564)

5 Elizabeth I ended any prospect of Mary marrying Leicester and being named her heir (1565)

6 **St Fridolin's Day**

Mary's friend, Mary Livingston, married John Sempill, later 4th Lord Sempill (1565)

MARCH

7   **St Thomas Aquinas' Day**

Mary went in state to open
Parliament, flanked by earls
of Huntly, Crawford and
Bothwell (1565)

8   **St Felix' Day**

Darnley signed a passport
permitting Moray to return
to Scotland (1565)

9   **Feast of the Forty Martyrs**

Riccio was dragged from
Mary's presence and
murdered (1566)

10 **St Kessog's Day (Scotland)**

Moray returned from being exiled after the Chaseabout Raid (1566)

11 **St Oswin's Day**

Mary and Darnley escaped from Holyroodhouse to Dunbar Castle after Riccio's murder (1566)

12 **St Gregory the Great's Day**

Parliament appointed Earl of Arran as Governor and Tutor to Mary (1543)

MARCH

13 St Kenocha's Day

Moray requested a passport
to enter England from Sir
William Cecil (1567)

14 St Matilda of Ringelheim's Day

John Knox, Protestant
evangelist, invited by
Scottish nobles to return to
Scotland (1557)

15 St Longinus' Day

Four Scottish nobles given
joint physical custody of the
young Mary (1543)

16 **St Boniface's Day**

Marie of Guise's remains
were shipped to France for
burial (1561)

17 **St Patrick's Day**

Mary issued a summons to
loyal subjects to attend her,
armed, at Dunbar (1566)

18 **St Cyril's Day**

Mary re-entered Edinburgh
at the head of her army
(1566)

MARCH

---

19 **St Joseph's Day**

Mary sent Prince James
under guard to Stirling
Castle to protection of Earl
of Mar (1567)

_____
_____
_____
_____
_____
_____
_____
_____

---

20 **St Cuthbert's Day**

Darnley swore to Privy
Council he had no part in
planning Riccio's murder
(1566)

_____
_____
_____
_____
_____
_____
_____
_____

---

21 **St Benedict of Monte
Cassino's Day**

Last day of Mary's two-
week stay at St Andrews
(1562)

_____
_____
_____
_____
_____
_____
_____

---

22   **St Basil of Ancyra's Day**

Mary stayed at Falkland
Palace (1562)

23   English Privy Council
advised Elizabeth I that
Mary and François II of
France were her mortal
enemies (1560)

24   **St Botolph's Day**

Mary agreed to Lennox's
demand that Bothwell
stand trial for Darnley's
murder (1567)

MARCH

25 **Feast of the Annunciation**

Marry arrived at Pitlethie House in Fife for a five-day stay (1563)

Easter Sunday – 1543, 1554

26 John Knox exiled from Frankfurt (1556)

Easter Sunday – 1559, 1570, 1581

27 James VI & I died at Theobalds in Hertfordshire, England (1625)

28 Mary secluded herself to pray for four hours on this Good Friday (1567)

_____

_____

_____

_____

_____

_____

_____

_____

_____

29 Sixty-eight men were attainted for their part in the murder of Riccio (1566)

Easter Sunday – 1551, 1562

_____

_____

_____

_____

_____

_____

_____

_____

_____

30 Mary responded to Elizabeth I's suggestion that she marry Leicester (1564)

Easter Sunday – 1567, 1578

_____

_____

_____

_____

_____

_____

_____

_____

MARCH

31 Henri II of France was born
(1519) and acceeded to the
throne (1547)

_____

_____

_____

_____

_____

_____

_____

_____

_____

Notes

_____

_____

_____

_____

_____

_____

_____

_____

_____

_____

_____

_____

_____

_____

_____

_____

_____

_____

Notes

MONTH PLANNER

April

1 Last day of Mary's ten-day stay at Falkland Palace (1562)

2 Duke of Norfolk led English troops into Scotland to support Lords of the Congregation (1560)

3 Countess of Lennox, Mary's aunt and mother-in-law, was buried (1578)

4 Mary signed secret documents making the French Crown her heir, should she have no issue (1558)

5 James VI left Edinburgh for London to take the English throne (1603)

6 Sir Francis Walsingham died (1590)

7 George Buchanan read Livy with Mary (1562)

8 Mary stayed at Falkland Palace (1563)

9 Mary wrote to John Spens about her fears of conspiracy (1565)

10 Lennox brought 10,000 men from Glasgow to Edinburgh for Bothwell's trial (1567)

11 Earl of Arundel, later suspected of involvement in the Throckmorton Plot, entered the English House of Lords (1581)

12 Parliament granted the regency to Marie of Guise (1554)

13 Catherine de' Medici, Queen of France, was born (1519)

14 Earl of Bothwell died insane, in Denmark (1578)

15 Lord James Stewart met Mary at St Dizier in north-eastern France (1561)

16 Mary stayed at Cupar in Fife (1563)

17 Lords of the Congregation signed a bond to expel the French from Scotland (1560)

18 Mary stayed at St Andrews (1563)

19 Mary betrothed to Dauphin François in a ceremony at the Louvre (1552)

20 Members of nobility and kirk signed Ainslie Bond, pledging to promote Bothwell's marriage to Mary (1567)

21 Mary was reconciled with earls of Moray and Argyll, after Chaseabout Raid (1566)

22 Sir William Kirkcaldy wrote to Earl of Bedford that Bothwell intended to abduct Mary (1568)

23 Mary left Stirling Castle after a three-day stay with Prince James; the last time she saw him (1567)

24 Mary married François, Dauphin of France, at Notre Dame, Paris (1558)

25 Diane de Poitiers, mistress of Henri II and a strong influence during Mary's life in France, died (1566)

26 Bothwell returned to Edinburgh, leaving Mary at Dunbar Castle (1568)

27 City of Aberdeen petitioned Mary for instruction on how to defend her against Bothwell (1567)

28 Elizabeth I, Queen of England, was buried at Westminster Abbey (1603)

29 Earls of Moray, Argyll and Glencairn appointed to Privy Council (1566)

30 All supporters of the King's Party were ordered to leave Edinburgh (1571)

Birthdays	Anniversaries	Reminders	Projects

Gardening	Events	Occasions	Festivals

MARY'S FIRST MARRIAGE

In 1543, Henry VIII arranged a marriage between the Queen of Scots and his son, Edward. The Treaty of Greenwich was signed on 1st July 1543 by the Governor of Scotland but its Parliament refused to ratify the treaty. Henri II of France suggested an alternative husband – his heir, François. Considering the French to be the lesser of two evils, Parliament accepted the Treaty of Haddington under which Mary was to be married to François on the condition Henri would defend Scotland as though it were his own territory, whilst respecting Scotland's independence. In 1548, five-year-old Mary said farewell to her mother and embarked for France where she took her place amongst the royal children, soon striking up a close friendship with François.

Mary's position as queen-regnant of Scotland was nowhere near so important, in French minds, as her role as a future consort of France, and it was the latter position for which she was educated. Scotland would be ruled by a French nominee, and then united with France through Mary's putative son.

Mary, fifteen, and François, fourteen, were betrothed on 10th April, 1558. The terms of the marriage treaty seemed reasonable. François was recognised as king of Scots, in right of his wife,

with the government to be carried on by Marie of Guise. State documents were to be signed by both. If Mary were to die childless, the throne would pass to her next Scottish heir. Once François acceded to the French throne, the countries would be ruled jointly, and their citizens would be naturalised in both countries. Their son would inherit both crowns, but, if they had only daughters, the eldest would become Queen of Scots.

So far, so good. But Mary was persuaded, or coerced, into signing three secret documents. These passed Scotland, in the event of her death without children, to France, together with her rights of inheritance in England. They also agreed that Scotland would repay the costs incurred by France in defending it and invalidated any future acts of Parliament which were in opposition to these articles. Mary probably genuinely believed that Scotland would benefit from being, effectively, an outpost of France.

The wedding, on 24th April, was elaborately celebrated. Contrary to custom, Mary wore white, the colour of mourning for French queens. Later, she may have regretted the unlucky choice. The marriage probably remained unconsummated before François' early death.

DUNBAR CASTLE

Mary stayed at Dunbar Castle, the closest royal fortress to Edinburgh, several times in the final turbulent years of her reign, and not always by choice.

Located on the coast some thirty miles to the east of Edinburgh, Dunbar Castle was a twelfth-century fortification, strategically located on a promontory by Dunbar harbour. Its site, surrounded by water on three sides, and massive stone structure, created a formidable defensive position. Originally the stronghold of the earls of Dunbar, it became a royal property in the mid-fifteenth century and was slighted in 1457 to prevent English occupation. Mary's grandfather, James IV, rebuilt it, and her mother, Mary of Guise, extended it substantially in the 1550s.

In March 1566, when Mary escaped from Holyroodhouse, where she was held captive by her Lords, following the murder of her secretary, David Riccio, she went to the safety of Dunbar Castle. The five-hour journey on horseback in the middle of the night was arduous for Mary, who was some six months pregnant at the time. She and Darnley remained at Dunbar for five days, mustering support, before going back to Edinburgh at the head of an 8,000-strong army.

Mary returned to Dunbar Castle the following year in even more difficult circumstances. On 24th April 1567 she was brought to the castle by the Earl of Bothwell, appointed Lieutenant of Dunbar Castle by Mary in reward for his support following Riccio's murder. Bothwell and 800 of his armed men had intercepted Mary on her journey from Linlithgow to Edinburgh. Once at the castle, according to contemporary sources, Bothwell held Mary captive and raped her. They left Dunbar on 5th May and headed for Edinburgh, where they were married on 15th May 1567. However, in dispute with the Lords, the couple retreated again to the safety of Dunbar Castle little more than one month later. After a four-day stay they headed, with a small armed escort, back to Edinburgh. On 15th June, two miles outside the city at Carberry Hill, they encountered the Lords and their armed supporters. Eventually, it was agreed that Mary would surrender to the Lords, and Bothwell would go free. He returned to Dunbar Castle briefly before fleeing Scotland for Norway.

Dunbar Castle was slighted again, on Parliament's order, in December 1567. Most of the ruins were removed in the nineteenth century, leaving today only the picturesque remains of a tower, courtyard and blockhouse.

APRIL

1 Last day of Mary's ten-day
stay at Falkland Palace
(1562)

Easter Sunday 1581, 1584

2 Duke of Norfolk led
English troops into Scotland
to support Lords of the
Congregation (1560)

Easter Sunday 1553, 1564

3 **St Richard of Chichester's
Day**

Countess of Lennox, Mary's
aunt and mother-in-law, was
buried (1578)

Easter Sunday 1575, 1580

4   **St Ambrose's Day**

Mary signed secret
documents making the
French Crown her heir,
should she have no issue
(1558)

5   James VI left Edinburgh
for London to take the
English throne (1603)

Easter Sunday 1545, 1556

6   **St Celestine's Day**

Sir Francis Walsingham
died (1590)

APRIL

7 George Buchanan read Livy
with Mary (1562)

8 Mary stayed at Falkland
Palace (1563)

9 Mary wrote to John Spens
about her fears of conspiracy
(1565)

10 Lennox brought 10,000 men from Glasgow to Edinburgh for Bothwell's trial (1567)

Easter Sunday 1547, 1559, 1569, 1583

11 **St Leo the Great's Day**

Earl of Arundel, later suspected of involvement in the Throckmorton Plot, entered the English House of Lords (1581)

12 Parliament granted the regency to Marie of Guise (1554)

APRIL

13 Catherine de' Medici,
Queen of France, was born
(1519)

Easter Sunday 1544

14 SS Tiberius, Valerian and
Maximus' Day

Earl of Bothwell died
insane, in Denmark (1578)

Easter Sunday 1555, 1560,
1566

15 St Magnus of Orkney's
Day

Lord James Stewart met
Mary at St Dizier in
north-eastern France (1561)

Easter Sunday 1571, 1582

16 Mary stayed at Cupar in
Fife (1563)

_____

_____

_____

_____

_____

_____

_____

_____

_____

17 **St Donanus' Day**

Lords of the Congregation
signed a bond to expel
the French from Scotland
(1560)

Easter Sunday 1552

_____

_____

_____

_____

_____

_____

_____

_____

18 Mary stayed at St Andrews
(1563)

Easter Sunday 1557, 1568

_____

_____

_____

_____

_____

_____

_____

APRIL

19 **Pope St Leo IX's Day**

Mary betrothed to Dauphin
François in a ceremony at
the Louvre (1552)

Easter Sunday 1579

20 Members of nobility and
kirk signed Ainslie Bond,
pledging to promote
Bothwell's marriage to
Mary (1567)

21 **St Anselm of Canterbury's
Day**

Mary was reconciled with
earls of Moray and Argyll,
after Chaseabout Raid
(1566)

Easter Sunday 1549

22 Sir William Kirkcaldy
wrote to Earl of Bedford
that Bothwell intended to
abduct Mary (1568)

Easter Sunday 1565, 1576

23 **St George's Day**

Mary left Stirling Castle
after a three-day stay with
Prince James; the last time
she saw him (1567)

24 **St Wilfrid of York's Day**

Mary married François,
Dauphin of France, at
Notre Dame, Paris (1558)

APRIL

25 St Mark the Evangelist's Day

Diane de Poitiers, mistress of Henri II and a strong influence during Mary's life in France, died (1566)

Easter Sunday 1546

26 SS Cletus and Marcellinus' Day

Bothwell returned to Edinburgh, leaving Mary at Dunbar Castle (1568)

27 St Anastasius's Day

City of Aberdeen petitioned Mary for instruction on how to defend her against Bothwell (1567)

28 **St Vitalus' Day**

Elizabeth I, Queen of
England, was buried at
Westminster Abbey (1603)

29 Earls of Moray, Argyll and
Glencairn appointed to
Privy Council (1566)

30 **St Catherine of Siena's
Day**

All supporters of the King's
Party were ordered to leave
Edinburgh (1571)

APRIL

Notes

Notes

MONTH PLANNER

May

1   Lords signed bond at Stirling to defend Prince James against Darnley's murderers (1567)

2   Mary escaped from captivity in Lochleven Castle (1568)

3   Lady Jean Gordon granted divorce from Bothwell in Protestant Kirk (1567)

4   Earls of Arran and Bothwell were imprisoned in Edinburgh Castle (1562)

5   James VI & I was buried in Henry VII Chapel at Westminster Abbey (1625)

6   Mary and Bothwell returned to Edinburgh after he held her captive at Dunbar Castle (1567)

7   Marriage of Bothwell and Lady Jean Gordon was annulled in Consistory Court of the Catholic Church (1567)

8   Proclamation of widespread support for Mary amongst nobility made in the Hamilton Bond (1568)

9   Marie of Guise and James V married by proxy at Châteaudun (1538)

10   Mob assembled in Perth in support of four Protestant preachers (1559)

11   John Knox's inflammatory preaching at Perth sparked iconoclastic riots (1559)

12   Banns of marriage for Mary and Bothwell were read (1567)

13   Mary's forces defeated by the rebel lords at Battle of Langside (1568)

14   Mary and Bothwell signed a marriage contract (1567)

15   Mary married Bothwell in a Protestant ceremony at Holyroodhouse (1567)

16   Mary crossed Solway Firth to England in a fishing boat (1568)

17   Earls of Lennox and Glencairn agreed to kidnap Mary and take her to Henry VIII (1544)

18   Second proxy wedding for James V and Marie of Guise held at Notre Dame (1538)

19   Elizabeth I ordered Mary's arrest (1568)

20   Mary wrote she was being well treated and expected to be back in Scotland at the head of an army around 15 August (1568)

21   Moray, angry at proposed marriage between Mary and Darnley, withdrew from court (1565)

22   A son, James, was born to James V and Marie of Guise (1540)

23   Duke of Châtelherault tried unsuccessfully to make peace with Darnley (1565)

24   Mary gave an audience in Paris to English ambassador, Throckmorton (1559)

25   Sir William Maitland went to London to arrange a meeting in York between Mary and Elizabeth I (1562)

26   The Kirk submitted requests to the Lords of the Council, including one to suppress idolatry (1561)

27   Marie of Guise negotiated with John Knox to enter Perth, following the rioting (1559)

28   Edinburgh Castle surrendered to troops of James VI, ending the war between the Queen's Party and the King's (1573)

29   Mary and François II ratified the Treaty of Upsettlington (Norham) (1559)

30   Charles IX of France died of tuberculosis (1574)

31   Lord James Stewart joined the Lords of the Congregation (1559)

Birthdays	Anniversaries	Reminders	Projects

Gardening	Events	Occasions	Festivals

ESCAPE FROM LOCHLEVEN

Mary and Bothwell confronted the rebel lords at Carberry Hill. Neither side was eager for battle, and during the day, there was much parleying back and forth. Eventually, Mary ended the stalemate by agreeing to stand her army down and go with the Confederate Lords, on condition of a safe-conduct for Bothwell.

Immediately, Mary's mistake became obvious. Far from being treated with respect, she was taken through the streets of Edinburgh to shouts of 'murderess' and 'whore'. She was then carried off to Lochleven castle, a fortress situated in the centre of a loch, and home of Lady Douglas, née Margaret Erskine, mother of her half-brother, Moray.

Whilst at Lochleven, Mary still refused to divorce Bothwell – presumably to preserve the legitimacy of the child she was carrying. She was harshly treated in Lochleven, and Elizabeth's ambassador, who was not permitted to see her, was appalled at the situation. He maintained that only his intervention, and the indication that Elizabeth would take Mary's death very badly, prevented the Lords from dispatching her. This cruel treatment no doubt contributed to the miscarriage of twins that Mary suffered in July. Whilst she was lying in her sickbed, she was bullied into signing articles of abdication. The Lords immediately moved to have the one-year-old James crowned. Cannon were fired at Lochleven in celebration. Subsequently, Mary maintained that the abdication was invalid, having been obtained by coercion.

Mary now recovered her energy and ingenuity. By dint of her charm, she persuaded Margaret's son, George Douglas, to smuggle out a letter to her supporters. Soon after, she made a first attempt at an escape, dressed as a laundress. The boatman became suspicious when he saw her beautifully-kept hands, and returned her to the castle shore. Perhaps pitying his queen, even if he did not want the responsibility of helping her escape, he kept her secret. Two weeks later, she made another attempt, and on 2nd May, Willie Douglas, nephew of Lady Margaret, sabotaged all the castle boats but one, and stole the keys from his cousin. Mary swapped clothes with her lady-in-waiting, Mary Seton, who stood in the window to attract attention, whilst Willie rowed Mary to shore, having locked the gates and hidden the castle keys. Once on the mainland, Mary was met with horses by George Douglas (stolen from Lochleven) and dashed for the Seton castle at Niddrie to consider her next move.

LOCHLEVEN CASTLE

Mary was held prisoner by the Confederate Lords at Lochleven Castle for almost a year and it is here that she abdicated in favour of her baby son.

Located on a small island in the middle of Loch Leven, it had been a royal castle in the fourteenth century and was used as a state prison by several monarchs before it was granted to the Douglas family. David II imprisoned his nephew, later Robert II, there, along with the latter's son, in 1368-9.

The island was smaller than it is today, consisting of little more than the walled castle enclosure and a small garden on a terrace to the north of the castle; the water would have lapped close to the curtain walls.

The thirteenth-century castle was in the possession of Sir William Douglas, half-brother of James, Earl of Moray, at the time of Mary's incarceration. Mary had been a guest of Sir William's at the castle several times before arriving as a prisoner. She visited in 1561 and again in 1565 with her husband, Lord Darnley. On one memorable occasion in 1563, she had a long religious debate in the Great Hall at Lochleven with John Knox, the Protestant reformer.

However, her experience as a prisoner was markedly different. Following her surrender at Carberry Hill, Mary was brought to Lochleven, on 17th June 1567, where she was held in harsh conditions. She miscarried of twins shortly after her arrival. In her resulting weakened state, she was forced by the Lords to sign a deed of abdication on 24th July 1567.

The tower house in which Mary was incarcerated dominates the castle's ruins. The bottom two floors contained kitchens and service areas. It is believed Mary's room was above the Great Hall, with a window that was converted into a small oratory for her private use. It is thought that the room above this, occupied by her doctor, is the one within which Mary changed into disguise for her escape.

On 2nd May 1568, Mary successfully escaped from Lochleven, on her second attempt, with the help of two of Sir William's younger brothers, making it across the loch by boat to support waiting on the mainland.

Today Lochleven is managed by Historic Environment Scotland. It is possible to visit between April and September, to cross the loch and to see the substantial remains of the tower house in which Mary was held.

MAY

1   **SS Philip and James the Less, the Apostles' Day**

Lords signed a bond at Stirling to defend Prince James against Darnley's murderers (1567)

2   Mary escaped from captivity in Lochleven Castle (1568)

3   **SS Alexander, Eventius and Theolous' Day**

Lady Jean Gordon was granted her divorce from James Hepburn, Earl of Bothwell in Protestant Kirk (1567)

MAY

4 **St Anthony of Tours' Day**

Earls of Arran and
Bothwell were imprisoned
at Edinburgh Castle (1562)

5 James VI & I was buried
in Henry VII Chapel at
Westminster Abbey (1625)

6 **St John the Evangelist's
Day**

Mary and Bothwell
returned to Edinburgh
after he held her captive at
Dunbar Castle (1567)

87

MAY

7 Marriage of Bothwell and
Lady Jean Gordon was
annulled in Consistory
Court of the Catholic
Church (1567)

_____
_____
_____
_____
_____
_____
_____
_____
_____

8 **Feast of the Archangel
Michael**

Proclamation of widespread
support for Mary amongst
the nobility made in the
Hamilton Bond (1568)

_____
_____
_____
_____
_____
_____
_____
_____

9 **St Nicholas of Myra's Day**

Marie of Guise married
James V by proxy at
Châteaudun (1538)

_____
_____
_____
_____
_____
_____
_____
_____

10 **St Aurelian of Limoge's Day**

Mob assembled in Perth in support of four Protestant preachers (1559)

11 **St Mamertus' Day**

John Knox's inflammatory preaching at Perth sparked iconoclastic riots (1559)

12 **SS Nereus and Achilleus' Day**

Banns of marriage for Mary and Bothwell were read (1567)

MAY

13   Mary's forces defeated by
the rebel lords at Battle of
Langside (1568)

14   **St Boniface's Day**

       Mary and Bothwell signed a
marriage contract (1567)

15   Mary married Bothwell in
a Protestant ceremony at
Holyroodhouse (1567)

16 Mary crossed Solway Firth to England in a fishing boat (1568)

17 Earls of Lennox and Glencairn agreed to kidnap Mary and take her to Henry VIII (1544)

18 Second proxy wedding for James V and Marie of Guise held at Notre Dame (1538)

MAY

19 **St Pudentiana's Day**

Elizabeth I ordered Mary's
arrest (1568)

20 Mary wrote she was being
well treated and expected to
be back in Scotland at the
head of an army around 15
August (1568)

21 Moray, angry at proposed
marriage between Mary and
Darnley, withdrew from
court (1565)

22 A son, James, was born
to James V and Marie of
Guise (1540)

23 Duke of Châtelherault tried
unsuccessfully to make
peace with Darnley (1565)

24 Mary gave an audience
in Paris to the English
ambassador, Throckmorton
(1559)

MAY

25 SS Gregory VII and Urban's Day

Sir William Maitland went to London to arrange a meeting in York between Mary and Elizabeth I (1562)

26 St Augustine of Canterbury's Day

The Kirk submitted requests to the Lords of the Council, including one to suppress idolatry (1561)

27

Marie of Guise negotiated with John Knox to enter Perth, following the rioting (1559)

28 St Bridget of Sweden's Day

Edinburgh Castle
surrendered to troops of
James VI, ending the war
between the Queen's Party
and the King's (1573)

29

Mary and François II
ratified the Treaty of
Upsettlington (Norham)
(1559)

30

Charles IX of France died
of tuberculosis (1574)

MAY

31 **St Petronilla's Day**

Lord James Stewart
joined the Lords of the
Congregation (1559)

Notes

MAY

Notes

MONTH PLANNER

June

1 A dying Marie of Guise sent for Lord James Stewart and other rebellious lords for reconciliation (1560)

2 Duke of Norfolk executed for treason, after planning to marry Mary (1572)

3 Mary went into confinement for birth of her child (1566)

4 Lord James Stewart and Earl of Argyll led armed force to join other Reformers at St Andrews (1560)

5 Earl of Huntly appointed Lord Chancellor (1546)

6 Scots nobles signed bond to promote marriage between Mary and Prince Edward of England (1543)

7 Earl of Bothwell moved Mary to Borthwick Castle (1567)

8 Marie of Guise made her will (1560)

9 Mary arrived for her week-long stay at Dunfermline Abbey (1562)

10 Lord James Stewart requested Mary's return from France (1561)

11 Marie of Guise, Regent of Scotland, died (1560)

12 Earls of Morton and Mar issued proclamation accusing Bothwell of 'ravishing' Mary (1567)

13 Earl of Ruthven, one of Riccio's assassins, died (1566)

14 Earl of Bothwell was at Haddington with 1,400 men (1568)

15 Mary surrendered to the lords at Carberry Hill (1567)

16 Marie of Guise arrived at Balcomie in Scotland from France (1538)

17 James V and Marie of Guise were married at St Andrews (1538)

18 Mary was imprisoned at Lochleven Castle (1567)

19 Mary's son, later James VI & I, was born (1566)

20 Countess of Lennox sent to Tower of London following the announcement of Darnley's betrothal to Mary (1565)

21 Mary stayed at Holyroodhouse (1563)

22 Mary stayed at Stirling Castle (1562)

23 Elizabeth I wrote to Mary, admonishing her for marrying Earl of Bothwell (1567)

24 Swedish ambassadors arrived, proposing Mary marry Prince Gustavus (1563)

25 Mary wrote her first letter to Anthony Babington (1586)

26 Perth surrendered to Marie of Guise's French-paid troops (1560)

27 Mary stayed at Stirling Castle (1562)

28 Cardinal of Guise told Mary of her mother's death (1560)

29 Mary accepted Sir William Maitland's service, but forbade him from passing information to England (1561)

30 Henri II of France wounded in a jousting match (1559)

Birthdays	Anniversaries	Reminders	Projects

Gardening	Events	Occasions	Festivals

BIRTH OF JAMES

When her secretary, Riccio, was murdered after being dragged from her presence, Mary was six months pregnant. To restrain her during the assassination, she had been held pinion by her husband, with a pistol aimed at her belly. Nevertheless, the following night she escaped, and rode the thirty miles to Dunbar Castle at a gallop. When she tried to slow down, warning Darnley that she might miscarry, he laughed at her fears, assuring her that if she did lose the baby, they could soon make another. Fortunately, she survived the ordeal, and did not go into labour until she was at full term, in the relative comfort and security of Edinburgh Castle.

It was, however, a long and painful birth, and Mary cried out that she was 'so sore handled' that she wished she had never been married. Worried that she would not survive, Mary made her will, probably appointing a regency council. Eventually, her son was born. The news was greeted with joy – the castle guns fired a salute, and bonfires were lit across the land. Throughout the last stages of her pregnancy, Mary had been careful to remain on good terms with her husband so that he would publicly affirm parentage of the baby. He came to her rooms and she said, in front of witnesses, 'this is your son, and no other man's

son'. Darnley accepted the child, then went out on one of his drinking sprees. Mary herself took a long time to recover physically from the birth, and perhaps psychologically, as well. The whole year since her marriage had been one crisis after another.

The baby was christened in December 1566 in a full Catholic ceremony. He was named Charles James – Charles for his godfather, King Charles IX of France, and James for his line of Stewart forebears. His godmother was Elizabeth I of England, who sent a font of solid gold. The christening was the most splendid event of Mary's reign and the only time she raised taxation for her own use, generally she supported herself and her government from Crown income and her dower from France. That Darnley refused to attend the ceremony, sulking outside, made little difference to anyone. Mary's chief goal now was to keep her son safe, and he was sent to the almost-impregnable Stirling Castle to be brought up by the Earl of Mar.

EDINBURGH CASTLE

Edinburgh Castle was a place of safety for Mary and her unborn son, after the murder of her private secretary and the turbulent events that followed.

Located at the top of the Royal Mile, the defensive advantages of the castle's site on a granite rock outcrop overlooking Edinburgh are obvious. However, James IV and James V increasingly favoured the more modern and comfortable royal palaces at Linlithgow, Stirling and Falkland and, once the Palace of Holyroodhouse was built, that became the primary royal residence in Edinburgh. Nevertheless, James IV undertook building works here, too, completing work on the main courtyard, the royal apartments and the Great Hall.

The castle was mainly used as a state armoury, prison, and for the safekeeping of records and other valuables; it continued to provide protection too. When the forces of Mary's mother, Marie of Guise, were besieged at Leith, she retreated to the castle, dying there on 11th June 1560. A heavily-pregnant Mary moved to the safety of the castle in April 1566, following Riccio's murder. She gave birth to her only child, James VI, in the royal apartments on 19th June 1566, and they remained at the castle until August 1566 when Mary moved baby James to Stirling Castle.

Most of the castle that Mary knew was destroyed in the 'Lang Siege' of 1568 – 1573. Heavy artillery fire demolished most of the medieval structure, although the sixteenth-century royal apartments, incorporating the birthing chamber where Mary bore James, survived. These lodgings and the Great Hall, with its magnificent hammerbeam roof, are all that remains from James IV's building programme. Visitors to them can also view the Honours of Scotland, the Scottish crown jewels – the oldest in Britain, they were used by Mary at her coronation. A replica set of 37 embroideries created by Mary during her exile in England are also displayed in the Royal Apartments.

Oliver Cromwell besieged the castle in 1650. Charles II subsequently undertook much new work on the fortifications and many of the present buildings date from the seventeenth and eighteenth centuries. Edinburgh Castle remains an active military base today, and it houses the National War Museum, two regimental museums and the Scottish National War Memorial. It is also home to the world-famous Edinburgh Military Tattoo, held in August each year.

Historic Environment Scotland manages the castle, which is open to the public throughout the year.

JUNE

1 **St Justin's Day**

A dying Marie of Guise
sent for Lord James Stewart
and other rebellious lords
for reconciliation (1560)

2 **St Peter and Marcellinus'
Day**

Duke of Norfolk executed
for treason, after planning
to marry Mary (1572)

3 Mary went into
confinement for birth of her
child (1566)

4 **St Petroc's Day**

Lord James Stewart
and Earl of Argyll led
armed force to join other
Reformers at St Andrews
(1560)

5 **St Boniface and
Companions' Day**

Earl of Huntly appointed
Lord Chancellor (1546)

6 Scots nobles signed bond to
promote marriage between
Mary and Prince Edward
of England (1543)

JUNE

7   **St Paul of Constantinople's Day**

Earl of Bothwell moved Mary to Borthwick Castle (1567)

8   Marie of Guise made her will (1560)

9   **SS Primus and Felicianus' Day**

Mary arrived for her week long stay at Dunfermline Abbey (1562)

JUNE

10 Lord James Stewart
requested Mary's return
from France (1561)

11 **St Basilides and
Companions' Day**

Marie of Guise, Regent of
Scotland, died (1560)

12 Earls of Morton and
Mar issued proclamation
accusing Bothwell of
'ravishing' Mary (1567)

JUNE

13 **St Anthony of Padua's Day**

Earl of Ruthven, one of
Riccio's assassins, died
(1566)

14 Earl of Bothwell was at
Haddington with 1,400
men (1568)

15 Mary surrendered to the
lords at Carberry Hill
(1567)

16 Marie of Guise arrived at
Balcomie in Scotland from
France (1538)

17 James V and Marie of
Guise were married at St
Andrews (1538)

18 **SS Marcus and
Marcellianus' Day**

Mary was imprisoned at
Lochleven Castle (1567)

JUNE

19 **SS Gervasius and Protasius' Day**

Mary's son, later James VI
& I, was born (1566)

20 **St Edward, King and Martyr's, Day**

Countess of Lennox sent to
Tower of London following
the announcement of
Darnley's betrothal to Mary
(1565)

21 Mary stayed at
Holyroodhouse (1563)

22 **St Alban's Day**

Mary stayed at Stirling
Castle (1562)

23 **St Etheldreda's Day**

Elizabeth I wrote to Mary,
admonishing her for
marrying Earl of Bothwell
(1567)

24 **St John the Baptist's Day**

Swedish ambassadors
arrived, proposing Mary
marry Prince Gustavus
(1563)

JUNE

25 Mary wrote her first letter
to Anthony Babington
(1586)

26 Perth surrendered to Marie
of Guise's French-paid
troops (1560)

27 **St Cyril of Alexandria's
Day**

Mary stayed at Stirling
Castle (1562)

28 **St Irenaeus' Day**

Cardinal of Guise told
Mary of her mother's death
(1560)

29 **Feast of SS Peter and Paul,
the Apostles**

Mary accepted Sir William
Maitland's service, but
forbade him from passing
information to England
(1561)

30 Henri II of France
wounded in a jousting
match (1559)

JUNE

Notes

JUNE

Notes

MONTH PLANNER

July

1 Treaty of Greenwich, requiring betrothal of Mary to Prince Edward of England, signed (1543)

2 Hearing of Mary's marriage to Bothwell, Pius V broke off diplomatic relations (1567)

3 Mary, recovering from illness, was taken into garden at Chartley Manor (1586)

4 Mary stayed at Stirling Castle (1562)

5 Treaty of Edinburgh, recognising Elizabeth I as Queen of England, signed by Scots Lords (1560)

6 James VI and Elizabeth I entered Treaty of Berwick, rendering Mary expendable (1586)

7 Treaty of Haddington, requiring betrothal of Mary and Dauphin François, was ratified (1548)

8 Safe-conduct drafted for Mary to travel to York to meet Elizabeth I (1563)

9 Sir Francis Walsingham wrote to Leicester that Mary would soon be caught plotting (1586)

10 Henri II of France died and Mary's husband ascended throne as François II (1559)

11 Mary travelled from Glasgow to Paisley for dinner (1563)

12 Elizabeth I postponed meeting with Mary, due to renewed war in France (1563)

13 Mary taken from Carlisle Castle, to be moved to Bolton Castle (1568)

14 Mary stayed at Stirling Castle (1562)

15 Mary arrived at Bolton Castle, where she was held for six months (1568)

16 Mary recalled Earl of Bothwell from France (1565)

17 Mary wrote to Anthony Babington tacitly condoning Elizabeth I's assassination (1586)

18 Protestant Lords suggested Earl of Arran and Elizabeth I marry and take Scottish throne (1560)

19 Lords of the Congregation requested English support against Marie of Guise (1559)

20 Mary attended four-day fete at St-Germain before departing for Scotland (1561)

21 Knox preached against Mary as 'whore of Babylon' and 'scarlet adventuress' (1567)

22 Banns read for Mary's wedding to Lord Darnley (1565)

23 Moray arrived in London to protest his innocence of Mary's mistreatment to Sir William Cecil and Elizabeth I (1567)

24 Mary was forced to abdicate (1567)

25 Mary left French court to return to Scotland (1561)

26 Marie of Guise moved baby Mary to the safety of Stirling Castle (1543)

27 Elizabeth I told Scots Lords she would not negotiate with them whilst they held Mary captive (1567)

28 Announced that Darnley would be King of Scots on his marriage to Mary (1565)

29 Mary's son was crowned King James VI (1567)

30 Mary's body was carried by night to Peterborough Cathedral, for burial (1587)

31 Moray left London for Scotland to install himself as regent (1567)

Birthdays	Anniversaries	Reminders	Projects

Gardening	Events	Occasions	Festivals

JOURNEY TO FRANCE

To foil the plans to kidnap Mary and take her to England that were allegedly being made by her great-uncle, Henry VIII, the 1548 Treaty of Haddington provided for her to be taken to France. Accordingly, aged just five, she was taken to Dumbarton Castle. Dumbarton, perched above the Clyde at Glasgow, is the oldest continuously-fortified stronghold in Britain. Once the centre of the kingdom of Strathclyde, in 1548 it was in the hands of the Earl of Arran, Governor of Scotland during Mary's minority. A troop of French soldiers was already in the castle, with provisions for a year, lest the English attack. With the queen were her nurse, her governess, Lady Fleming, several of her half-siblings, including Lord James Stewart, and her four friends, all named Mary – Beaton, Seton, Fleming and Livingston.

On 29th July, Mary said goodbye to her mother and embarked on the French royal galley. Immediately, storms blew up and the flotilla was damaged whilst still at anchor. Mary proved an excellent sailor, and like all those to whom sea-sickness is unknown, remarkably unsympathetic to sufferers. Her strong stomach served her well on the eighteen day rough passage to St-Pol-de-Léon in Brittany. As soon as the fleet landed, word was sent to Henri II, and to Mary's maternal grandparents, Charles, Duke of Guise and his duchess, Antoinette de Bourbon. The cavalcade made for Nantes, where they embarked on barges to carry them down the Loire to the chateau of St-Germain-en-Laye. Having just recovered from the sea journey, a number of the entourage now fell ill, probably with food-poisoning, and one, the brother of Mary Seton, died.

Antoinette de Bourbon was delighted with her granddaughter, praising her looks, her grace and her deportment. She was less impressed with Mary's attendants, observing that some of them were not as clean as they might have been – a harsh judgement after several weeks of sea-journey and travel.

Just outside St-Germain, Mary met the 'enfants de France' – her betrothed, the dauphin, the princesses, Elisabeth and Claude, and Prince Louis. She was to be brought up with them, and to share a room with Elisabeth, although, as a sovereign queen, Mary had precedence over everyone except Henri II, his queen, Catherine de' Medici, and the dauphin. Arriving a few days later, Henri was delighted with Mary, and, despite her youth, she was soon participating in the magnificent rituals of the French court.

BOLTON CASTLE

Mary spent six months when she arrived in England at Bolton Castle, before she was moved further south to Tutbury Castle.

Located in Wensleydale, North Yorkshire, Bolton Castle is a well-preserved medieval fortress that was also a luxurious residence, built by Richard, 1st Baron Scrope of Bolton, powerful Lord Chancellor and Lord Treasurer to Richard II, at the end of the fourteenth century. Facing south over the Yorkshire Dales, it has commanding views, ideal for a castle only 80 miles from what was then the Scottish border, and subject to numerous raids from the Scots and from border reivers.

Mary had been in England less than two months, staying briefly at Workington Hall and Carlisle Castle, when she was brought to Bolton, escorted by Sir Francis Knollys on 15th July 1568. She stayed there for six months in total before she was taken to Tutbury Castle in Staffordshire. It was during her time at Bolton that Mary's trial for the murder of her second husband, Lord Darnley, was held in York and then Westminster. Mary was not permitted to attend, nor to see any of the evidence brought against her.

Built of Yorkshire sandstone, Bolton has a square floor plan with a central courtyard created by four tall ranges with an enormous towers in each of the four corners. The south-west tower contained the principal lodgings of the Scrope family that Mary, as a high-status guest, used. On the first floor the solar, designated as Mary's privy chamber, is where she would have spent most of her days, in writing, needlework and learning to read and write in English, under the tutelage of Sir Francis Knollys. The adjoining hall, today known as the Great Chamber, was where Mary dined, under her cloth of state. Lady Scrope's bedchamber was on the second floor and Lord Scrope's bedchamber, assigned to Mary for the duration of her stay, was on the third floor.

Although partially slighted during the English Civil War, Bolton is remarkably well-preserved and the part of the castle containing the high-status rooms which Mary would have used, remains broadly complete.

The castle is still in the private ownership of Lord Bolton, a direct descendant of its original owner, Sir Richard le Scrope. It is open to visitors year-round.

JULY

1 **Octave of Feast of St John the Baptist**

Treaty of Greenwich, requiring betrothal of Mary to Prince Edward of England, signed (1543)

2 **The Feast of the Visitation**

Hearing of Mary's marriage to Bothwell, Pius V broke off diplomatic relations (1567)

3 Mary, recovering from illness, was taken into garden at Chartley Manor (1586)

JULY

4 **St Ulrig of Augsburg Day**

Mary stayed at Stirling
Castle (1562)

5 Treaty of Edinburgh,
recognising Elizabeth I as
Queen of England, signed
by Scots Lords (1560)

6 **Octave of Feast of SS Peter
and Paul**

James VI and Elizabeth
I entered into Treaty of
Berwick, rendering Mary
expendable (1586)

JULY

7 Treaty of Haddington, requiring betrothal of Mary and Dauphin François, was ratified (1548)

8 **St Elizabeth of Portugal's Day**

Safe-conduct drafted for Mary to travel to York to meet Elizabeth I (1563)

9 **Octave of the Visitation**

Sir Francis Walsingham wrote to Leicester that Mary would soon be caught plotting (1586)

10 SS Rafina and Secunda's Day

Henri II of France died and Mary's husband ascended throne as François II (1559)

11 St Benedict's Day

Mary travelled from Glasgow to Paisley for dinner (1563)

12 SS Nabor and Felix's Day

Elizabeth I postponed meeting with Mary, due to renewed war in France (1563)

JULY

13 Mary taken from Carlisle
Castle, to be moved to
Bolton Castle (1568)

14 Mary stayed at Stirling
Castle (1562)

15 **St Swithun's Day**

Mary arrived at Bolton
Castle, where she was held
for six months (1568)

16 Mary recalled Earl of Bothwell from France (1565)

17 **St Alexius' Day**

Mary wrote to Anthony Babington tacitly condoning Elizabeth I's assassination (1586)

18 **St Edburga's Day**

Protestant Lords suggested Earl of Arran and Elizabeth I marry and take Scottish throne (1560)

July

19 **St Arsenius' Day**

Lords of the Congregation
requested English support
against Marie of Guise
(1559)

_____

_____

_____

_____

_____

_____

_____

_____

20 **St Margaret of Antioch's Day**

Mary attended four-day
fete at St-Germain before
departing for Scotland
(1561)

_____

_____

_____

_____

_____

_____

_____

21 Knox preached against
Mary as 'whore of Babylon'
and 'scarlet adventuress'
(1567)

_____

_____

_____

_____

_____

_____

_____

22   **St Mary Magdalene's Day**

Banns read for Mary's
wedding to Lord Darnley
(1565)

23   **St Apollinarus' Day**

Moray arrived in London
to protest his innocence
of Mary's mistreatment
to Sir William Cecil and
Elizabeth I (1567)

24   **St Christina's Day**

Mary was forced to abdicate
(1567)

JULY

25 **Feast of the Apostle James the Great**

Mary left French court to return to Scotland (1561)

26 **St Anne's Day**

Marie of Guise moved baby Mary to the safety of Stirling Castle (1543)

27 Elizabeth I told Scots Lords she would not negotiate with them whilst they held Mary captive (1567)

28 St Panatleon's Day

Announced that Darnley
would be King of Scots
on his marriage to Mary
(1565)

29 St Martha's Day

Mary's son was crowned
King James VI (1567)

30 SS Abdon and Sennen's Day

Mary's body was carried
by night to Peterborough
Cathedral, for burial (1587)

July

31 St Fabius' Day

Moray left London for
Scotland to install himself
as regent (1567)

Notes

Notes

MONTH PLANNER

August

1 Mary ordered rebellious Moray to appear before her within six days (1565)

2 Sir Francis Walsingham's assistant requested instructions for apprehending Anthony Babington (1586)

3 Marie of Guise's French relatives sent money to support her regency (1559)

4 Sir William Maitland reconciled to Mary after Riccio's murder and re-appointed as Secretary (1566)

5 Sir Nicholas Throckmorton believed Mary, having miscarried, would divorce Bothwell (1568)

6 Moray outlawed for his rebellion against Mary's marriage to Darnley (1565)

7 Mary set sail from Dumbarton for France, with her friends, the Four Marys (1548)

8 Mary requested Elizabeth I to grant her safe passage from France (1561)

9 Sir Nicholas Throckmorton met Mary in Paris and was impressed by her (1560)

10 Mary arrived at Calais, en route home to Scotland (1561)

11 Mary led her army north to subjugate rebellious Gordon clan (1562)

12 Funeral oration for Marie of Guise in Notre Dame (1560)

13 Mary and her Four Marys landed near Roscoff, in France (1548)

14 Anthony Babington was arrested (1586)

15 A priest celebrating Mass in Mary's chapel in her absence was attacked (1562)

16 Papal jurisdiction rejected, and Catholic Mass outlawed in Scotland (1560)

17 English sighted Mary's flotilla off Flamborough Head (1561)

18 Mary landed at St-Pol-de-Leon in Brittany, France (1548)

19 Mary landed in Leith, Scotland; returning to begin her personal rule (1561)

20 Mary stayed in Perth (1562)

21 Mary stayed at Coupar Angus Abbey (1562)

22 Earl of Moray proclaimed as Regent of Scotland (1568)

23 Mary travelled from Glamis Castle to Edsell Castle (1562)

24 Mary heard first Mass of her personal rule in her private chapel (1561)

25 Mary issued proclamation forbidding religious changes until Parliament made a final order (1561)

26 Mary's muster to capture Moray was completed, after she had sold her jewels to pay the troops (1565)

27 Mary and her army arrived at Aberdeen, where Lady Huntly pleaded for her son, accused of treason (1562)

28 Mary led her army out of Edinburgh to capture Moray and his fellow rebels (1565)

29 Sir William Cecil informed Knox using alias 'Sinclair' during his illegal sojourn in Berwick (1559)

30 Mary stayed in Aberdeen (1562)

31 Edinburgh's Provost welcomed Mary to the city (1561)

Birthdays	Anniversaries	Reminders	Projects

Gardening	Events	Occasions	Festivals

THE QUEEN'S RETURN

After the death of her husband, François II, in 1560, Mary informed her Scots nobles that she was considering returning to Scotland. In fact, her preferred option was a marriage to Don Carlos, son of Philip II of Spain. Her mother-in-law, Catherine de' Medici, was secretly opposed to this, and wrote to her daughter, Elisabeth, Philip's wife, that she should discourage the match.

Simultaneously, Mary was trying to build bridges with Elizabeth I of England, whilst delaying ratifying the Treaty of Edinburgh. She did not wish formally to accept Elizabeth as queen of England, until Elizabeth accepted her as the legitimate heir. Mary told Elizabeth's envoy, Sir Thomas Randolph, that she needed to consult with her Council before she could commit herself. In the meantime, she expressed her warm wishes towards her cousin, and hoped that they might meet in person to resolve any disputes.

Whilst contemplating her future, Mary visited her Guise relatives – possibly because Catherine had made it clear that she was not welcome at court. According to Sir James Melville, Catherine was 'rigorous and vengeable' towards her daughter-in-law.

Two embassies arrived from Scotland – one under the leadership of John Leslie,

the Catholic Bishop of Ross, and the other led by Mary's half-brother, Lord James Stewart. Leslie had the direst suspicions of Lord James – certain that he coveted his sister's throne. He recommended that Mary have James detained, and embark for Scotland to raise an army in the Catholic Highlands, to impose her will. Mary rejected Leslie's advice and agreed to Lord James' suggestion that she return home, under the condition that she accept Protestantism as Scotland's religion, whilst she maintained her own Catholic religion in private.

Agreement made, Mary requested a passport from Elizabeth to travel through England. It was refused, but Mary set sail anyway, on 14th August, 1561 landing at Leith five days later on a day of miserable fog and gloom. She had docked earlier than anticipated and there was a mad dash to Leith by the welcoming committee. The populace was delighted at the sight of their beautiful young queen and lit bonfires to express public satisfaction in her arrival. In honour of her arrival, music was played outside her palace chamber at Holyroodhouse. The French envoy, M. de Brantôme, complained about the appalling noise, but Mary was probably thrilled that her people were so welcoming, and requested a repeat performance the next day.

FALKLAND PALACE

Falkland Palace, a popular country residence of the Stewart kings from the mid-fifteenth century, was also favoured by Mary, who used it regularly.

James II confiscated the thirteenth-century castle at Falkland from the Earl of Fife in the fifteenth century and Mary's grandfather and father subsequently transformed it into a Renaissance palace. James IV undertook extensive building works to the palace, adding the south and east ranges (containing the new royal lodgings), to create three ranges around an open courtyard.

James V carried out substantial works, embellishing his father's buildings with decorations inspired by a chateau he visited during his time in France. Indeed, Falkland Palace is considered one of first true Renaissance buildings in Britain.

It was to Falkland that James V retreated following his army's defeat by the English at the Battle of Solway Moss, and he died there less than three weeks later, in December 1542.

Falkland was a convenient stopping off point for Mary's visits to Perth and St Andrews and she also often stayed for several weeks at a time in the spring. The opportunities for falconry, hawking

and hunting in the extensive parkland and forests surrounding Falkland added substantially to its appeal for Mary, who was a keen participant in these activities. She also enjoyed playing tennis, using the real (royal) tennis court that her father had built there the year before he died. This court remains today, the world's oldest real tennis court still in use.

Mary's son, James VI, used Falkland Palace until he gained the English Crown in 1603, and moved south to London. When Falkland was occupied by the soldiers of Oliver Cromwell in the 1650s, a fire started which partially destroyed the palace, and it subsequently fell into ruin. In the late nineteenth century the palace was rescued and restored by the 3rd Marquess of Bute. Today it is possible to see the roofed south range, containing the Chapel Royal, and the east range containing the royal lodgings, with their reproduction sixteenth-century furnishings, painted ceilings and royal arms.

Falkland Palace is managed by the National Trust of Scotland and open to visitors throughout much of the year.

AUGUST

1 **Feast of the Maccabees**

Mary ordered rebellious
Moray to appear before her
within six days (1565)

2 **Pope St Stephen I's Day**

Sir Francis Walsingham's
assistant requested
instructions for
apprehending Anthony
Babington (1586)

3 **St Walthen of Melrose's Day**

Marie of Guise's French
relatives sent money to
support her regency (1559)

4 Sir William Maitland
reconciled to Mary after
Riccio's murder and
re-appointed as Secretary
(1566)

5 Sir Nicholas Throckmorton
believed Mary, having
miscarried, would divorce
Bothwell (1568)

6 **Feast of the
Transfiguration**

Moray outlawed for his
rebellion against Mary's
marriage to Darnley (1565)

AUGUST

7 **St Sixtus II and Companions' Day**

Mary set sail from Dumbarton for France, with her friends, the Four Marys (1548)

8 **St Cyriacus and Companions' Day**

Mary requested Elizabeth I grant her safe passage from France (1561)

9 Sir Nicholas Throckmorton met Mary in Paris and was impressed by her (1560)

10 **St Lawrence's Day**

Mary arrived at Calais, en
route home to Scotland
(1561)

11 Mary led her army north to
subjugate rebellious Gordon
clan (1562)

12 **St Clare's Day**

Funeral oration for Marie
of Guise in Notre Dame
(1560)

AUGUST

13 Mary and her Four Marys landed near Roscoff, in France (1548)

_____

14 **Vigil of the Assumption of the Blessed Virgin**

Anthony Babington was arrested (1586)

_____

15 **Assumption of the Blessed Virgin**

A priest celebrating Mass in Mary's chapel in her absence was attacked (1562)

_____

16 Papal jurisdiction rejected, and Catholic Mass outlawed in Scotland (1560)

17 **Octave of St Lawrence**

English sighted Mary's flotilla off Flamborough Head (1561)

18 **St Helena's Day**

Mary landed at St-Pol-de-Leon in Brittany, France (1548)

AUGUST

19 Mary landed in Leith,
Scotland; returning to begin
her personal rule (1561)

20 St Bernard's Day

Mary stayed in Perth (1562)

21 Mary stayed at Coupar
Angus Abbey (1562)

22 **Octave of the Assumption**

Earl of Moray proclaimed
as Regent of Scotland
(1568)

23 Mary travelled from
Glamis Castle to Edsell
Castle (1562)

24 **St Bartholomew the
Apostle's Day**

Mary heard first Mass of
her personal rule in her
private chapel (1561)

AUGUST

25 **St Louis IX's Day**

Mary issued proclamation
forbidding religious changes
until Parliament made a
final order (1561)

---

26 Mary's muster to capture
Moray was completed, after
she had sold her jewels to
pay the troops (1565)

---

27 Mary and her army arrived
at Aberdeen, where Lady
Huntly pleaded for her son,
accused of treason (1562)

28 St Augustine of Hippo's Day

Mary led her army out of Edinburgh to capture Moray and his fellow rebels (1565)

29

Sir William Cecil informed Knox using alias 'Sinclair' during his illegal sojourn in Berwick (1559)

30 SS Felix and Adauctus' Day

Mary stayed in Aberdeen (1562)

AUGUST

31 Edinburgh's Provost
welcomed Mary to the
city (1561)

Notes

Notes

MONTH PLANNER

September

1   Sir Richard Knightley, witness to the executions of Babington and Mary, died (1615)

2   Mary's state entry to Edinburgh after her return from France dazzled the populace (1561)

3   Rival claimants for governorship, the Earl of Arran and Cardinal Beaton, compromised (1543)

4   Earl of Lennox, regent for his grandson, James VI, killed in an affray (1571)

5   Mary was at Holyroodhouse (1561)

6   Bothwell appointed to Mary's new Privy Council (1561)

7   Duke of Norfolk arrested for involvement in Ridolfi Plot (1571)

8   Arran repudiated English alliance and was reconciled to Catholic Church (1543)

9   Mary was crowned Queen of Scots at Stirling Castle (1543)

10   English defeated Scots at the Battle of Pinkie Cleugh (1547)

11   Mary began her first royal progress in Scotland (1561)

12   Mary's supporters challenged authenticity of the Casket Letters (1568)

13   Mary stayed at Inverness Castle in the Scottish Highlands (1562)

14   Mary's chapel was stormed whilst she was hearing Mass (1561)

15   Mary and Catherine de' Medici granted Sir Nicholas Throckmorton an interview (1559)

16   Mary wrote to her mother of the sudden deaths of several of the Scots embassy (1559)

17   Mary arrived at Spynie for a two-night stay at palace of Bishop of Moray (1562)

18   François II was crowned King of France at Rheims Cathedral (1559)

19   Following dinner at Cullen, Mary travelled to Boyne Castle for the night (1562)

20   Anthony Babington and his co-conspirators were executed (1586)

21   Mary entered Angers on her journey from Scotland to French court (1548)

22   Lennox returned to Edinburgh after long exile in England (1564)

23   Bothwell submitted to Mary after his escape from captivity (1562)

24   Mary stayed in Aberdeen (1562)

25   Mary reunited with Marie of Guise at Rouen (1550)

26   Mary was at Stirling Castle (1563)

27   Mary stayed in Aberdeen (1562)

28   Mary stayed at Falkland Palace in Fife (1561)

29   Lennox informed Mary that Darnley felt so humiliated he would leave Scotland (1566)

30   Mary asked Darnley, in front of her Council, to explain why he was so offended (1566)

Birthdays	Anniversaries	Reminders	Projects

Gardening	Events	Occasions	Festivals

MARY'S CORONATION

Not long before the Scottish Parliament refused to ratify the Treaty of Greenwich, which would have married Mary to Prince Edward of England, the year-old queen was moved from Linlithgow to Stirling, accompanied by the earls of Huntly, Lennox, Argyll and Bothwell.

Stirling Castle was one of the most formidable fortresses in Scotland and although the English attempted several schemes to abduct Mary, they were not practicable, and, so long as she remained there and the castle was not directly attacked by an invading army, she was safe. Stirling was also one of the most splendid of the Scottish royal palaces and Mary and her mother, the dowager-queen, Marie of Guise, lived there in comfort and ease. Marie's chief ambition was to see her daughter crowned, and to maintain the French alliance.

On 9th September 1543 the first of these desires was accomplished when Mary was crowned as the first queen-regnant in the British Isles, in the Chapel Royal at Stirling. It was not an auspicious day to have chosen, being the thirtieth anniversary of the crushing defeat that Mary's grandfather, James IV, had suffered at the hands of the English at Flodden. Nor was there much money to spare for a grand ceremony – the English ambassador, Sadler reported

it as 'not very costlie'. Nevertheless, its performance enhanced Mary's position. The 'honours of Scotland', as the royal regalia are known, were borne by three earls – Governor Arran carried the crown, the Earl of Argyll the sword and the Earl of Lennox the sceptre. This was the first occasion recorded on which all three pieces were used together. The crown had been made for Mary's father, James V, to wear at the coronation of Marie of Guise as consort. Naturally, with Mary being only an infant, it could not be placed on her head, so it was held over her by Cardinal Beaton, who officiated. He anointed Mary with the holy oil. Unaware of the importance of the ceremony, nine-month old Mary howled all the way through. Undaunted, the nobles – or at least those who supported the French alliance, knelt and swore allegiance. Supporters of the English alliance stayed away. To shorten the ceremony to reflect Mary's age, the usual reading of the royal genealogy was foregone. After the crowning was over, the court danced, masqued and feasted in Stirling's Great Hall. Three months after, Parliament confirmed the Auld Alliance with France.

STIRLING CASTLE

Stirling Castle was Mary's childhood home before she left Scotland for the French court.

The castle is perched on an outcrop of volcanic rock in the heart of Scotland where the Highlands meet the Lowlands. This strategic location, close to the Firth of Forth, overlooks the site of both the Battle of Bannockburn (1314), and the Battle of Sauchieburn (1488).

In the half-century before Mary's birth, the castle's collection of buildings had been the subject of extensive renovations and new construction by her grandfather, James IV, and father, James V. These extensions included the King's Old Building, the Great Hall, and the Foreworks, all in the latest Renaissance styles.

Mary was brought to the safety of Stirling from her birthplace at Linlithgow Palace when she was seven months old. A few months later, in September 1543, baby Mary was crowned in the Chapel Royal, the church founded by her grandfather, James IV. She was briefly moved to Inchmahome Priory on an island in the Lake of Menteith for a few weeks in September 1547, when the 'Rough Wooing' of the English brought them as far as Edinburgh following the disastrous defeat of the Scots at the Battle of Pinkie Cleugh.

On her return from France, Mary visited Stirling frequently during the years of her personal rule, spending weeks at a time there most years. She brought her baby son, Prince James, to Stirling after his birth at Edinburgh Castle and his baptism in the Chapel Royal was followed by a three day long celebration – the most sumptuous of her reign.

The Chapel Royal looked very different in Mary's day – then, it was a Catholic chapel with all the typical ornamentation, stained glass and relics. With the Protestant Reformation, these were stripped away, and the Chapel today is a much plainer space.

However, the main palace block has been restored to look much as it would have done when Mary's mother, Marie of Guise, was Regent of Scotland, whilst Mary herself was in France. The decoration is very colourful and vibrant, with carved and painted wooden ceilings and expensive tapestries and wall hangings.

Stirling Castle, managed by Historic Environment Scotland, is open to visitors throughout the year.

SEPTEMBER

1 **St Priscus' Day**

Sir Richard Knightley,
witness to the executions of
Babington and Mary, died
(1615)

2 Mary's state entry to
Edinburgh after her return
from France dazzled the
populace (1561)

3 **St Gregory the Great's Day**

Rival claimants for
governorship, the Earl of
Arran and Cardinal Beaton,
compromised (1543)

4 **St Cuthbert's Day**

Earl of Lennox, regent for
his grandson, James VI,
killed in an affray (1571)

5 Mary was at
Holyroodhouse (1561)

6 Bothwell appointed to
Mary's new Privy Council
(1561)

SEPTEMBER

7 **Vigil of the Nativity of the Blessed Virgin**

Duke of Norfolk arrested for involvement in Ridolfi Plot (1571)

8 **Feast of the Nativity of the Blessed Virgin**

Arran repudiated English alliance and reconciled to Catholic Church (1543)

9 Mary was crowned Queen of Scots at Stirling Castle (1543)

10 English defeated Scots at
Battle of Pinkie Cleugh
(1547)

11 Mary began her first royal
progress in Scotland (1561)

12 Mary's supporters
challenged authenticity of
the Casket Letters (1568)

SEPTEMBER

13 Mary stayed at Inverness Castle in Scottish Highlands (1562)

14 Mary's chapel was stormed whilst she was hearing Mass (1561)

15 **Octave of the Nativity of the Blessed Virgin**

Mary and Catherine de' Medici granted Sir Nicholas Throckmorton an interview (1559)

16 **SS Cornelius and Cyprian's Day**

Mary wrote to her mother of the sudden deaths of several of the Scots embassy (1559)

17 **St Lambert's Day**

Mary arrived at Spynie for a two night stay at palace of Bishop of Moray (1562)

18 François II was crowned King of France at Rheims Cathedral (1559)

SEPTEMBER

19 Following dinner at Cullen, Mary travelled to Boyne Castle for the night (1562)

20 Anthony Babington and his co-conspirators were executed (1586)

21 **St Matthew the Apostle's Day**

Mary entered Angers on her journey from Scotland to French court (1548)

22 Lennox returned to
Edinburgh after a long exile
in England (1564)

_____
_____
_____
_____
_____
_____
_____
_____
_____

23 **St Thecla's Day**

Bothwell submitted to
Mary after his escape from
captivity (1562)

_____
_____
_____
_____
_____
_____
_____

24 **Feast of the Conception of
St John the Baptist**

Mary stayed in Aberdeen
(1562)

_____
_____
_____
_____
_____
_____

SEPTEMBER

25 Mary reunited with Marie
of Guise at Rouen (1550)

26 St Cyprian's Day

Mary was at Stirling Castle
(1563)

27 Mary stayed in Aberdeen
(1562)

28 St Wenceslaus of
Bohemia's Day

Mary stayed at Falkland
Palace in Fife (1561)

29 Feast of St Michael and
All Angels (Michaelmas)

Lennox informed Mary
that Darnley felt so
humiliated he would leave
Scotland (1566)

30 St Jerome's Day

Mary asked Darnley, in
front of her Council, to
explain why he was so
offended (1566)

September

Notes

Notes

MONTH PLANNER

October

1 Mary ordered Border lords to attend her at Melrose for a justice-in-ayre (1566)

2 Rumour in England James V was declining to meet Henry VIII until Marie of Guise had borne her child (1542)

3 Parliament ordered all smaller benefices to be granted to Protestants (1566)

4 Scotland retained Julian calendar when Gregorian calendar was introduced (1582)

5 Sadler reported Marie of Guise so well guarded it would be impossible to kidnap her (1543)

6 Elizabeth I told Mary to prepare herself for trial (1586)

7 Margaret Douglas, Countess of Lennox, was born (1515)

8 Judges who were to try Mary assembled in London (1586)

9 Mary stayed in Aberdeen (1562)

10 Elizabeth I taken ill with smallpox (1562)

11 Moray showed the Casket Letters to English commissioners (1568)

12 Edward VI of England was born (1537)

13 Randolph reported Mary and Darnley were quarrelling over her refusal to give him the Crown Matrimonial (1565)

14 Mary agreed to participate in her own trial (1586)

15 Mary's two-day trial began (1586)

16 Mary and her court visited Bothwell, recovering from an injury at Hermitage Castle (1566)

17 Mary was at Holyroodhouse (1561)

18 Fearful of assassination, François II and Mary went to Orléans (1560)

19 Mary returned to Edinburgh following Chaseabout Raid (1565)

20 Duke of Guise, Mary's grandfather, was born (1496)

21 Duke of Châtelherault suspended Marie of Guise's position as regent (1559)

22 Darnley reported to be trying to oust Protestants from Privy Council (1566)

23 Mary wrote of her satisfaction nothing had been proved against her at York (1568)

24 Marie of Guise deposed from regency by Lords of the Congregation (1559)

25 Mary pronounced guilty of treason by commission in London, after her trial (1586)

26 Mary gravely ill at Jedburgh (1566)

27 John Knox wrote an angry letter to Lords of the Congregation (1557)

28 Earl of Huntly's revolt against Mary was defeated at Corrichie (1562)

29 John Knox forced to apologise to English government for leak of secret information (1559)

30 Mary's lodging at Jedburgh partially destroyed by fire (1566)

31 Elizabeth I secretly sent funds to Lords of the Congregation (1559)

Birthdays	Anniversaries	Reminders	Projects

Gardening	Events	Occasions	Festivals

THE JUSTICE-IN-AYRE

On 8th October 1566, Mary took one of the customary journeys of the Stewart monarchs, a 'justice-in-ayre' which was a peregrination around major towns to fulfil the ancient monarchical role of law- and justice-giver. In England, the role of judge had long been delegated from the sovereign to professional judges, but in Scotland, it remained an important part of monarchy. Day-to-day matters of justice were dealt with in the barons' courts, where the baron, or laird, had 'right of pit and gallows' and jurisdiction over 'life and limb', whilst the monarch heard more serious matters.

Mary would travel to the 'caput' or main town in the various sheriffdoms and hear the most serious cases. The sessions typically lasted from four to seven days, with Sundays always excluded, and on this occasion, Mary was making a circuit in Teviotdale and Liddesdale. These districts were in the Borders, and hence the Earl of Bothwell was the local lieutenant responsible for organising the circuit. The first session was held in Jedburgh.

At the time, prison as a punishment was almost unknown. The pannel (accused) would be held in the sheriff's gaol, until trial. If he were filed (convicted) his punishment would be either physical – hanging or the stocks – or

being outlawed for a sum of money. Additionally, criminal justice was not just a matter between the Crown and the wrong-doer, but was also a matter for the victim. The criminal would need to compensate the victim (or his family) through assythment, for which he would have to find sureties until it was paid. Once assythment had been agreed, the malefactor would be outlawed for that sum and the monarch would grant a pardon, conditional on the compensation being paid. An important part of the system was the use of sureties. These were the kinsmen and the laird of the pannel, who would also come into the court and, collectively, assume responsibility.

The justices-in-ayre were not generally courts for the finding of guilt; instead, pannels who had agreed assythment were brought forward for pardon, and to be brought back into the queen's mercy.

Following completion of the session at Jedburgh, Mary and the court visited Bothwell, who had been injured in an ambush. A day or two after her return, Mary fell seriously ill, possibly from a gastric ulcer perforating, precipitated by the sixty-mile return journey to see Bothwell.

TUTBURY CASTLE

Mary detested Tutbury Castle, one of the properties in which she spent a considerable amount of time as a prisoner.

A large medieval fortress of Norman origins, Tutbury's strategic site, high above the River Dove, contributed to its tumultuous history of rebellion, siege and rebuilding. The seat of the de Ferrers family and then the earls and dukes of Lancaster, it came into the ownership of the monarch at the turn of the fifteenth century when Henry Bolingbroke, son of John of Gaunt and Blanche of Lancaster, became Henry IV.

The castle reached its high point under the Lancastrian kings and much of the castle that remains today is from that time. By the mid-sixteenth century, Tutbury was 'decayed in many places' and in need of major repair. However, its location, in the English Midlands, was conveniently remote from both Elizabeth I's base in London, and support from northern England and Scotland, to keep the captive queen.

Mary arrived at Tutbury for the first time in February 1569 and she hated it. The ageing castle was damp, draughty, and cold. Furnishings had been hastily sent from Sheffield, but could not hide the stench from the latrines underneath her chamber windows. She was moved to Wingfield Manor in June 1569, to avoid suspected rescue attempts, and then back to Tutbury again a few months later. However, when events leading to the Rising of the North created further concerns, Mary was moved further south to Coventry in November 1569. Once the rebellion had been thwarted, she was moved back to Tutbury in January 1570 and remained there for another five months.

Mary spent the next fifteen years in Sheffield, Wingfield and other properties of her gaoler, George Talbot, Earl of Shrewsbury. She moved back to Tutbury for the final time, in January 1585, under the care of her new gaoler, Sir Ralph Sadler, Chancellor of the Duchy of Lancaster, and remained there until December 1585, when she was taken to Chartley Manor.

Tutbury Castle was slighted on the orders of Parliament during the Commonwealth and although some repairs were made following the Restoration, it remains substantially in ruins today.

Tutbury continues to be in the ownership of the Duchy of Lancaster, the private estate of HM The Queen. It is open for events and activities year round, and on a seasonal basis to the general public.

OCTOBER

1   Mary ordered Border lords
to attend her at Melrose for
a justice-in-ayre (1566)

2   Rumour in England James
V was declining to meet
Henry VIII until Marie of
Guise had borne her child
(1542)

3   Parliament ordered all
smaller benefices to be
granted to Protestants
(1566)

4 **St Francis of Assisi's Day**

Scotland retained Julian calendar when Gregorian calendar was introduced (1582)

5 Sadler reported Marie of Guise so well guarded it would be impossible to kidnap her (1543)

6 **St Faith's Day**

Elizabeth I told Mary to prepare herself for trial (1586)

OCTOBER

7   **SS Marcellus and Apulcius' Day**

Margaret Douglas, Countess of Lennox, was born (1515)

8   Judges who were to try Mary assembled in London (1586)

9   Mary stayed in Aberdeen (1562)

10 Elizabeth I taken ill with smallpox (1562)

11 Moray showed the Casket Letters to English commissioners (1568)

12 St Wilfred of York's Day

Edward VI of England was born (1537)

13 Randolph reported
Mary and Darnley were
quarrelling over her refusal
to give him the Crown
Matrimonial (1565)

14 Mary agreed to participate
in her own trial (1586)

15 **St Wulfram of Sens' Day**

Mary's two-day trial began
(1586)

16 Mary and her court visited Bothwell, recovering from an injury at Hermitage Castle (1566)

17 **St Ignatius Norono's Day**

Mary was at Holyroodhouse (1561)

18 **St Luke the Evangelist's Day**

Fearful of assassination, François II and Mary went to Orléans (1560)

OCTOBER

19 Mary returned to
Edinburgh following
Chaseabout Raid (1565)

_____
_____
_____
_____
_____
_____
_____
_____
_____

20 Duke of Guise, Mary's
grandfather, was born (1496)

_____
_____
_____
_____
_____
_____
_____
_____
_____

21 **Feast of the Eleven
Thousand Virgins**

Duke of Châtelherault
suspended Marie of Guise's
position as regent (1559)

_____
_____
_____
_____
_____
_____
_____

22 Darnley reported to be trying to oust Protestants from Privy Council (1566)

23 Mary wrote of her satisfaction nothing had been proved against her at York (1568)

24 Marie of Guise deposed from regency by Lords of the Congregation (1559)

OCTOBER

25 SS Crispin and
Crispinian's Day

Mary pronounced guilty
of treason by commission
in London, after her trial
(1586)

26 Mary was gravely ill at
Jedburgh (1566)

27 Vigil of Feast of SS Simon
and Jude

John Knox wrote an angry
letter to Lords of the
Congregation (1557)

28 **Feast of SS Simon and Jude, Apostles**

Earl of Huntly's revolt against Mary was defeated at Corrichie (1562)

29 John Knox forced to apologise to English government for leak of secret information (1559)

30 Mary's lodging at Jedburgh partially destroyed by fire (1566)

OCTOBER

31 All Hallow's Eve

Elizabeth I secretly sent
funds to Lords of the
Congregation (1559)

Notes

Notes

MONTH PLANNER

November

1   Mary argued with Sir Amyas Paulet, her final gaoler, over religion (1586)

2   Mary was prostrated after she attended hanging of Sir John Gordon (1563)

3   English Warden of the March told Duke of Suffolk about his attempt to burn Selkrig (1543)

4   Marie of Guise processed through London to dine with Edward VI (1551)

5   Mary left Aberdeen and travelled to stay at Dunnottar Castle (1562)

6   Lords of the Congregation forced to retreat from Edinburgh (1559)

7   Mary left Dunnottar Castle and travelled to Craig Castle (1562)

8   Bishop of Ross gave English Council details of Mary's plan to marry Norfolk (1571)

9   Bothwell challenged Arran to a duel after intercepting funds sent from Elizabeth I (1559)

10   Mary granted a passport to her friend, Lord Seton, to return to France (1560)

11   Mary stayed at Arbroath in Angus (1562)

12   English Parliament urged Elizabeth I to consent to Mary's execution (1586)

13   Sir James Melville of Halhill, Mary's ambassador to Elizabeth I, died (1617)

14   Bishop of Winchester begged Cecil to end his custodianship of Mary's representative, the Bishop of Ross (1573)

15   Mary stayed at Perth in Perthshire (1562)

16   François II was struck with terrible earache (1560)

17   Mary I of England died and Elizabeth I ascended the throne (1558)

18   Roberto di Ridolfi, merchant, banker and conspirator, was born (1531)

19   Robert Beale delivered death sentence to Mary at Fotheringhay Castle (1586)

20   Mary arrived at Craigmillar Castle to discuss problem of Darnley with her lords (1566)

21   Mary stayed at Linlithgow Palace in West Lothian (1562)

22   Likely birth date of Marie of Guise (1515)

23   Elizabeth I rejected Mary's request to re-negotiate Treaty of Edinburgh (1560)

24   John Knox, clergyman and Reformer, died (1572)

25   Commission of Westminster opened (1568)

26   Moray publicly accused Mary of Darnley's assassination (1568)

27   Sir Nicholas Throckmorton wrote to Elizabeth I that François II was unlikely to live (1560)

28   Mary agreed to abandon all claims to Scottish and English crowns in return for her freedom (1584)

29   Parliament voted to grant Crown Matrimonial of Scotland to Mary's husband, Dauphin François (1558)

30   Sir William Kirkcaldy offered to spy for England against France and Scotland (1556)

Birthdays	Anniversaries	Reminders	Projects

Gardening	Events	Occasions	Festivals

THE CRAIGMILLAR BOND

By the autumn of 1566, Mary was in despair over the behaviour of her husband, who was now trumpeting that he planned to go abroad. This would have been an embarrassment to Mary and Scottish government – an uncontrollable Darnley, roaming Europe and claiming to be hard-done-by would be a disaster. On 20th November, she and her councillors met at Craigmillar Castle on the outskirts of Edinburgh to discuss the matter. Technically, there might have been an annulment of the marriage, as it had taken place prior to Mary receiving papal dispensation for a marriage to her cousin. The problem with this option was that it might cloud the legitimacy of Prince James. Why Mary did not go down the route her great-uncle, Henry VIII, had paved, by having her husband arrested on a charge of treason and legally dispatched is a mystery – Darnley certain had given her plenty of ammunition, not least his involvement in the murder of Riccio.

In a report made many years later by the Earl of Huntly, five of her lords agreed at Craigmillar that Mary should be approached again about a divorce or annulment – those in favour were the earls of Moray, Huntly, Argyll, Morton and Bothwell, but Mary was reluctant. She was in the middle of tricky negotiations with Elizabeth I of England and did not want scandal to disrupt the draft treaty. Huntly then continued that Mary's secretary, Sir William Maitland, suggested that her councillors would find another way of dealing with the problem, and that if Moray did not agree the route forward then he would 'look through his fingers thereto and will behold our doings, saying nothing to the same'. Alarmed by this, Mary replied, 'I will that ye do nothing whereto any spot may be laid to my honour or conscience, and therefore I pray you rather let the matter be in the state as it is'. Maitland quickly reassured her that she would see nothing but 'good and approved by Parliament'. Nothing further was said at the time to Mary, but, again according to Huntly, he, along with Argyll, Morton, Maitland and Bothwell, signed a bond (which, if it ever existed, no longer does), agreeing to remove Darnley permanently, although it did not say how. The bond ended, according to Huntly, with the words 'or what other ways to dispatch him, which altogether Her Grace refuses, as is widely known'.

SHEFFIELD CASTLE AND MANOR

Mary spent the majority of her captivity, some fourteen years in total, at Sheffield Castle and its associated estates.

Sheffield Castle, in South Yorkshire, was a very substantial thirteenth-century castle, believed to have covered some four acres in total, situated in the 2,500 acres of Great Sheffield Park. Owned by Mary's gaoler, George Talbot, 6th Earl of Shrewsbury, it was considerably more comfortable for Mary than Tutbury Castle. Surrounded by a deep ditch on two sides and by the rivers Don and Sheaf on the others, it was also a formidable fortress which offered many advantages in the quest to keep Mary securely imprisoned.

More appealingly for Mary, Shrewsbury also owned a manor house, built by his grandfather, the 4th Earl of Shrewsbury, in 1516, in Great Sheffield Park and Mary was housed in both, moving between them as they required cleaning. The manor house was extended and improved in the early 1570s for Mary's use, including the construction of Turret House, a combined gatehouse and hunting tower, located in the perimeter wall. The three-storey Turret House had gate-keeper's lodgings on the ground floor, two floors of rooms probably used for banquets and entertainment, and a flat roof from which it was possible to see the countryside for miles around.

The castle was held by royalist forces during the Civil War and slighted soon after its surrender to Parliament. Too damaged to rebuild, the owner, the 22nd Earl of Arundel (grandson of the 6th Earl of Shrewsbury), demolished the remaining structure. Relatively little is known about the castle's composition or plan and no drawings or plans have been found to date. However, archaeological work suggests that remains of the castle survive below an extensive area of Sheffield city centre and efforts are being made to undertake further excavation work.

The ruins of the manor house, including elements of the long gallery, and the Turret House, which Mary would have known, were sold by the Duke of Norfolk to Sheffield City Council in 1953. Now named Sheffield Manor Lodge, it is open to visitors on a seasonal basis.

NOVEMBER

1 **All Hallows' Day**

Mary argued with Sir
Amyas Paulet, her final
gaoler, over religion (1586)

_____

_____

_____

_____

_____

_____

_____

_____

_____

2 **All Souls' Day**

Mary was prostrated after
she attended hanging of Sir
John Gordon (1563)

_____

_____

_____

_____

_____

_____

_____

_____

3 English Warden of the
March told Duke of Suffolk
about his attempt to burn
Selkrig (1543)

_____

_____

_____

_____

_____

_____

_____

_____

4 Marie of Guise processed
through London to dine
with Edward VI (1551)

5 Mary left Aberdeen
and travelled to stay at
Dunnottar Castle (1562)

6 **St Leonard's Day**

Lords of the Congregation
forced to retreat from
Edinburgh (1559)

NOVEMBER

7   Mary left Dunnottar Castle
and travelled to Craig
Castle (1562)

8   **Feast of the Four Crowned
Martyrs**

Bishop of Ross gave English
Council details of Mary's
plan to marry Norfolk
(1571)

9   Bothwell challenged Arran
to a duel after intercepting
funds sent from Elizabeth I
(1559)

10 Mary granted a passport to
her friend, Lord Seton, to
return to France (1560)

11 St Martin of Tours' Day
(Martinmas)

Mary stayed at Arbroath in
Angus (1562)

12 St Macarius' Day

English Parliament urged
Elizabeth I to consent to
Mary's execution (1586)

13   St Brictius' Day

Sir James Melville of
Halhill, Mary's ambassador
to Elizabeth I, died (1617)

_____
_____
_____
_____
_____
_____
_____
_____

14   Bishop of Winchester
begged Cecil to end his
custodianship of Mary's
representative, the Bishop of
Ross (1573)

_____
_____
_____
_____
_____
_____
_____

15   Mary stayed at Perth in
Perthshire (1562)

_____
_____
_____
_____
_____
_____
_____

16   St Margaret of Scotland's Day

François II was struck with terrible earache (1560)

17   St Hilda of Whitby's Day

Mary I of England died and Elizabeth I ascended the throne (1558)

18   Octave of Martinmas

Roberto di Ridolfi, merchant, banker and conspirator, was born (1531)

November

19 **St Elizabeth's Day**

Robert Beale delivered
death sentence to Mary at
Fotheringhay Castle (1586)

20 Mary arrived at Craigmillar
Castle to discuss problem
of Darnley with her lords
(1566)

21 **St Columban's Day**

Mary stayed at Linlithgow
Palace in West Lothian
(1562)

22 **St Cecilia's Day**

Probable birth date of
Marie of Guise (1515)

23 **Pope St Clement I's Day**

Elizabeth I rejected Mary's
request to re-negotiate
Treaty of Edinburgh (1560)

24 **St Crisogonus' Day**

John Knox, clergyman and
Reformer, died (1572)

NOVEMBER

25 **St Catherine of Alexandria's Day**

Commission of Westminster opened (1568)

26 **St Conrad of Constance's Day**

Moray publicly accused Mary of Darnley's assassination (1568)

27 **SS Vitalis and Agricola's Day**

Sir Nicholas Throckmorton wrote to Elizabeth I that François II was unlikely to live (1560)

28 Mary agreed to abandon all claims to Scottish and English crowns in return for her freedom (1584)

_____
_____
_____
_____
_____
_____
_____
_____

29 **Vigil of St Andrew the Apostle**

Parliament voted to grant Crown Matrimonial of Scotland to Mary's husband, Dauphin François (1558)

_____
_____
_____
_____
_____
_____
_____

30 **Feast of St Andrew the Apostle**

Sir William Kirkcaldy offered to spy for England against France and Scotland (1556)

_____
_____
_____
_____
_____
_____
_____

NOVEMBER

Notes

Notes

MONTH PLANNER

December

1 Mary sent Elizabeth I a portrait of herself (1560)

2 Mary vomited 'a great quantity of corrupt blood' (1566)

3 Lords of the Congregation constituted themselves by signing a bond (1557)

4 Mary publicly declared guilty of treason against Elizabeth I (1586)

5 François II of France died (1560)

6 James V fell ill following Battle of Solway Moss (1542)

7 Moray produced Casket Letters at York-Westminster Commission (1568)

8 Mary was born at Linlithgow Palace in West Lothian (1542)

9 York-Westminster Commission reviewed Casket Letters (1568)

10 Parliament deferred Marie of Guise's claim for possession of Kirkwall Castle (1543)

11 Parliament refused to ratify treaty with England, annulling Mary's betrothal to Prince Edward (1543)

12 Lord Lisle reported to Henry VIII that Mary was weak and unlikely to survive (1542)

13 Parliament confirmed restoration of Earl of Lennox's Scottish estates (1564)

14 James V died at Falkland Palace (1542)

15 Scotland signed a treaty renewing Auld Alliance with France (1543)

16 John Knox appointed minister to English Protestant church in exile in Geneva (1558)

17 Prince James baptised in Chapel Royal at Stirling Castle (1566)

18 Earl of Arran wrote to Paul III regarding priory of Blantyre (1543)

19 Lennox wrote of Mary's pregnancy to his wife, imprisoned in Tower of London (1565)

20 Henry VIII of England sent messenger to Scotland to declare war (1543)

21 Catherine de' Medici became Regent of France for her son, Charles IX (1560)

22 François Clouet, who painted Mary at the court of France, died (1572)

23 François II was buried in royal abbey at St. Denis (1560)

24 Mary was moved from Tutbury Castle, for the last time (1585)

25 Earl of Bedford reported Mary and Darnley no longer on good terms (1565)

26 Cardinal Charles de Guise died (1574)

27 Sir William Cecil persuaded English Privy Council to intervene in Scottish Civil War (1559)

28 Mary dined at Haddington, then travelled to Dunbar Castle, East Lothian (1562)

29 Mary stayed at Dunbar Castle (1562)

30 Duke of Suffolk wrote to pro-English lords in Scotland advising them how to deal with Cardinal Beaton (1543)

31 Earl of Morton was arrested for complicity in the murder of Darnley (1580)

Birthdays	Anniversaries	Reminders	Projects

Gardening	Events	Occasions	Festivals

Mary's Birth

Mary was the daughter of James V of Scotland and his second wife, Marie of Guise. She was born at the delightful Renaissance palace of Linlithgow on 8th December 1542. Her parents had already had two sons who had tragically died within days of each other before Mary was born, she was thus immediately heir to the throne. As Marie laboured in childbirth, James lay mortally ill, probably with dysentery contracted following the disastrous Battle of Solway Moss where the English had inflicted a heavy defeat on the Scots. On being told of Mary's birth, he despaired, saying 'it cam' wi' a lass, and it will gang wi' a lass', referring to the Stewart inheritance of the Crown through Marjorie, daughter of Robert the Bruce.

Within a week, James was dead, Mary was queen and the country was in turmoil. Scotland and England remained at war. The leader of the English forces, John Dudley, Viscount Lisle, wrote to Mary's great-uncle, Henry VIII of England, for instructions, thinking it dishonourable to pursue a military offensive against a country whose king was dead and whose ruler was a 'young suckling'. Henry, although not particularly concerned about the chivalrous treatment of his great-niece, did cease overt military operations.

The Scots immediately sought to appoint a governor. This was not straightforward as the court was riddled with factions. The first candidate, according to custom, was Mary's nearest male heir, James Hamilton, 2nd Earl of Arran. Despite his royal connections, Arran, who leant towards Protestantism, was not widely respected – he was not especially intelligent, and he was extremely indecisive. His chief rival was Cardinal David Beaton. Beaton had been one of James's closest advisers and he claimed that James had left a will appointing him as governor, with four others to share the guardianship of the queen. Arran and the other nobles claimed the will was a forgery. Arran and Beaton disagreed on policy – Arran wanted a compromise with England, whilst Beaton preferred the ancient Franco-Scottish, Catholic, alliance.

There was a further claim to the governorship from Matthew Stuart, Earl of Lennox, based on his contention that the Earl of Arran was illegitimate. Lennox, whose father had been killed by Arran's, had spent most of his life in France, and was a protégé of François I.

Arran was confirmed as governor of Scotland in January 1543 and within days Cardinal Beaton was arrested.

LINLITHGOW PALACE

Mary was born at Linlithgow, the red stone Renaissance palace much favoured by the Stewart queens, as was her father, James V.

Located equidistant between the fortresses of Stirling Castle to the west and Edinburgh Castle to the east, Linlithgow Palace was a royal pleasure palace, used by the Stewarts as a convenient base for hunting and recreation.

The original royal manor house on the site burnt down in a major fire in 1424 that also seriously damaged Linlithgow town. James I rebuilt in stone – initially three ranges around a central courtyard. This building was added to, and remodelled by, subsequent monarchs during the fifteenth and sixteenth centuries, creating an impressive Renaissance palace. James IV added a fourth range, the northern range, with royal apartments for his new bride, Margaret Tudor, sister of Henry VIII. It was here, in the queen's privy apartments, that James V was born in 1512.

James V constructed the three-tier fountain which remains in the courtyard and the outer gateway at the entrance to the palace.

James V's second wife, Marie of Guise, gave birth to Mary, their third child, on 8th December 1542, probably in the same north-west tower in which he was born.

A few days later Mary was christened in St Michael's Church, located adjacent to the palace. And within the week, news arrived that James V had died, and the new-born Mary was now Queen of Scots.

Mother and child remained at Linlithgow until later in 1543, when they moved to the more secure location of Stirling Castle.

Mary returned to Linlithgow several times during her personal rule in the 1560s. She had just left Linlithgow, bound for Edinburgh, in March 1567, when the Earl of Bothwell intercepted her and took her to Dunbar Castle.

The palace was little used following the accession of Mary's baby son, James VI, and the north range collapsed in 1607. It was rebuilt on James VI's orders in 1620. However, Charles I was the last monarch to sleep there, in 1633.

The Duke of Cumberland and his soldiers stopped at the palace on their way to the Battle of Culloden (1746), left their fires burning on departure and the old palace was gutted.

Although ruinous, much of the impressive structure of Linlithgow Palace remains standing today, managed by Historic Environment Scotland and open to visitors year-round.

December

1 Mary sent Elizabeth I a
portrait of herself (1560)

2 **St Bibianus' Day**

Mary vomited 'a great
quantity of corrupt blood'
(1566)

3 Lords of the Congregation
constituted themselves by
signing a bond (1557)

4 **St Barbara's Day**

Mary was publicly declared
guilty of treason against
Elizabeth I (1586)

5 François II of France died
(1560)

6 **St Nicholas' Day**

James V fell ill following
Battle of Solway Moss
(1542)

December

7 **St Ambrose's Day**

Moray produced Casket
Letters at York-Westminster
Conference (1568)

8 **Feast of the Conception of
the Blessed Virgin**

Mary was born at
Linlithgow Palace in West
Lothian (1542)

9 York-Westminster
Commission reviewed
Casket Letters (1568)

10 Parliament deferred
Marie of Guise's claim
for possession of Kirkwall
Castle (1543)

11 St Damasus' Day

Parliament refused to
ratify treaty with England,
annulling Mary's betrothal
to Prince Edward (1543)

12 St Columba's Day

Lord Lisle reported to
Henry VIII that Mary
was weak and unlikely to
survive (1542)

DECEMBER

13 **St Lucy's Day**

Parliament confirmed
restoration of Earl of
Lennox's Scottish estates
(1564)

_____
_____
_____
_____
_____
_____
_____
_____

14 **St Erkenwald's Day**

James V died at Falkland
Palace (1542)

_____
_____
_____
_____
_____
_____
_____
_____

15 Scotland signed a treaty
renewing Auld Alliance
with France (1543)

_____
_____
_____
_____
_____
_____
_____
_____

16 John Knox appointed
minister to English
Protestant church in exile
in Geneva (1558)

17 Prince James baptised in
Chapel Royal at Stirling
Castle (1566)

18 Earl of Arran wrote to
Paul III regarding priory of
Blantyre (1543)

December

19 Lennox wrote of Mary's
pregnancy to his wife,
imprisoned in Tower of
London (1565)

20 Henry VIII of England sent
messenger to Scotland to
declare war (1543)

21 **St Thomas the Apostle's
Day**

Catherine de' Medici
became Regent of France for
her son, Charles IX (1560)

22 **SS Cyril and Methodius' Day**

François Clouet, who painted Mary at the court of France, died (1572)

23 François II was buried in royal abbey at St. Denis (1560)

24 **Vigil of the Nativity of Christ**

Mary was moved from Tutbury Castle for the last time (1585)

December

25 **Nativity of Christ (Christmas)**

Earl of Bedford reported Mary and Darnley were no longer on good terms (1565)

26 **St Stephen's Day**

Cardinal Charles de Guise died (1574)

27 **St John the Apostle's Day**

Sir William Cecil persuaded English Privy Council to intervene in the Scottish Civil War (1559)

28 Feast of the Holy Innocents

Mary dined at Haddington,
then travelled to Dunbar
Castle, East Lothian (1562)

29 St Thomas Becket's Day

Mary stayed at Dunbar
Castle (1562)

30 Feast of King David

Duke of Suffolk wrote
to pro-English lords in
Scotland advising them on
how to deal with Cardinal
Beaton (1543)

DECEMBER

31 Earl of Morton was arrested
for complicity in the murder
of Darnley (1580)

Notes

Notes

INDEX OF PEOPLE

Stewart was the spelling used by all members of the Scottish royal house until Mary's reign. The Lennox branch settled in France and used the spelling Stuart, this was thus the form used by Mary's second husband, Henry Stuart, Lord Darnley. Mary adopted this French form, and it was used by her and her descendants. Royalty are listed under first names. Women are listed under the better known of their maiden or married names.

Babington, Anthony (1561–1586) He first met Mary when a page in the Shrewsbury household, and after going to Paris, acted for a short time as a courier for Mary to the Catholic priest, Thomas Morgan. In 1584 he was talked into a plot for the assassination of Elizabeth I and her replacement with Mary. The English government was aware of the conspiracy, and perhaps incited it. Babington was arrested, tried, and hanged, drawn and quartered for treason

Beale, Robert (1541–1601) An associate of Sir Francis Walsingham, he became clerk to the English Privy council and negotiated on its behalf with Mary. Despite their differences she gave him a valuable golden chain.

Beaton, Cardinal David (c. 1494–1546) Beaton worked closely with James V and negotiated the king's marriage to Marie of Guise. Appointed as cardinal in 1538, and Archbishop of St Andrew's in 1539, he tried to stamp out early Protestantism. A rival for the regency in Mary's childhood, he became a target for the pro-English, pro-Protestant party and was assassinated at St Andrews.

Beaton, Mary, Lady Ogilvie (c. 1543–1597) was Mary's companion from early childhood. Daughter of a Scots noble and one of Marie of Guise's ladies, she accompanied Mary to France, where she was brought up at the Abbey of Poissy. Returning to Scotland with Mary, she married Alexander Ogilvy of Boyne and had two children.

Bothwell, Adam, Bishop of Orkney (c. 1521–1593) Connected to the professional elite of Edinburgh, and to the earls of Caithness, Bothwell may have been educated in France.

He was provided to the See of Orkney in 1559. Despite early difficulties, he established himself as a firm proponent of Protestantism and contributed to the Book of Discipline. Although he crowned Prince James, he never recovered from the disgrace of performing Mary's marriage to the Earl of Bothwell (no relation).

Bourbon, Antoinette de, Duchess of Guise (1494–1583) A descendant of European royal houses, Antoinette married Claud, Duke of Guise, an intimate of François I of France. They had numerous children and built a strong power base at the French court, although they were resented by many. Antoinette influenced Mary's childhood in France.

Bourdeilles, Pierre de, M. de Brantôme (c. 1540–1614) His family were courtiers to Marguerite, Queen of Navarre, sister of François I. He served in the French army both against external armies and during the Wars of Religion – generally supporting the Catholic side, but influenced by the Huguenots. He accompanied Mary on her return to Scotland in 1561 and his memoirs are a useful historical source.

Buchanan, George (1506–1582) Educated in France, he served with the Duke of Albany against the English. He graduated in Paris, then returned to Scotland where he began writing and turned to Protestantism. Later, he taught in Portugal, and was imprisoned for heresy, then spent more time in Italy and France before joining Mary's court. He read Livy with Mary, of whom he initially spoke well, but he blamed her for Darnley's death, and wrote tracts condemning her. He was appointed as tutor to James VI.

Carlos, Don, Prince of Spain (1545–1568)
Son of Philip of Spain and Maria Manuela of Portugal, he was mentally unstable from an early age – possibly caused by his having only six different great-grandparents, rather than the usual 16. Mary sought him as a second husband, but his condition was such that no marriage was possible.

Charles IX, King of France (1550–1574)
Inheriting the throne, aged ten, Charles was at the mercy of the warring factions at the French court. His mother, Catherine de' Medici, who acted as regent, sought to contain Catholic-Huguenot tensions, but failed. His reign saw the Massacre of St Bartholomew.

Clouet, François, (c. 1524–1572) Painter-in-ordinary to the kings of France, he depicted the royal family and chief nobles. He drew Mary as a child, in chalk, and painted her as an adult at least once.

Campbell, Archibald, 5th Earl of Argyll (d. 1558) Argyll's wealth and the extent of his estates made him one of the greatest magnates in the whole of the British Isles. He was married to Lady Jean Stewart, half-sister to Mary and to Moray, an unhappy union which Mary worked with Knox to reconcile. He and Moray were friends and associates, leading the Lords of the Congregation but after the Chaseabout Raid he was reconciled to Mary and presided over the court that acquitted Bothwell of Darnley's murder. He was to lead Mary's troops at Langside, but collapsed in the saddle, probably of a heart-attack, contributing to her defeat. He became a pillar of Morton's regency.

Catherine de' Medici, Queen of France (1519–1589) Catherine, niece of Pope Clement VII, was unhappily married to Henri II. On his death in 1559 she vied with the Guise family for influence in the reign of her son, François II. On his death she made it clear that Mary was no longer welcome in France. She assumed the regency for Charles IX, then Henri III. Despite her efforts to mediate the Wars of Religion, her actions contributed significantly to the Massacre of St Bartholomew.

Cecil, William, 1st Baron Burghley (1520–1598) William Cecil first came to prominence in the reign of Edward VI as Secretary to Lord Protector Somerset, then to the Privy Council as a whole. On Elizabeth's accession, he was appointed Secretary, and remained her most important and influential councillor until his death. Elizabeth was attached to him personally, as well as politically. Cecil saw Mary as the greatest enemy of the English state and never ceased planning her destruction.

Charles of Guise, Cardinal (1524–1574)
Mary's maternal uncle, he strongly influenced her childhood and, together with his brother, François, Duke of Guise, dominated the reign of François II. The main object of the family, of which he was the mastermind, was to dominate French politics – contributing to the vicious Wars of Religion.

Cunningham, William, 3rd Earl of Glencairn (d. 1548) Captured by the English at Solway Moss, he was 'persuaded' to support English interests in Scotland in return for his freedom and a pension. He promoted the marriage of Mary to Edward of England, and secretly agreed that, in the event of the queen's death, Scotland would be surrendered to Henry VIII. He vacillated in his loyalties, fighting for Scotland at Ancrum Moor, but continuing to flirt with the English.

Douglas, Archibald, 6th Earl of Angus (1489–1557) Second husband of Mary's grandmother, Margaret, Dowager-queen of Scots, Angus dominated James V's minority and was exiled as soon as James had the power to do so. Angus threw in his lot with Henry VIII of England, but eventually returned to Scottish allegiance, leading the victory at Ancrum Moor. His grandson, Lord Darnley, was Mary's second husband.

Douglas, George (d. after 1568) Maternal half-brother of Moray, he orchestrated Mary's successful escape from Lochleven and followed her into exile in England.

Douglas, James, 4th Earl of Morton (c. 1516–1581) Morton initially supported the Lords of the Congregation, but was equivocal in religion. He helped Mary in her defeat of Huntly and was apponted Chancellor. In 1565, he was persuaded to accept Mary's marriage to Darnley after Lady Lennox renounced her claims to the Douglas inheritance of Angus. He was a ringleader in the murder of Riccio. Later, he initially supported Mary's marriage to Bothwell, but turned against them. He became regent for James VI, but was eventually executed for complicity in Darnley's murder.

Douglas, Margaret, Countess of Lennox (1515-1578) Daughter of the the marriage of Margaret Tudor, Queen of Scots and the Earl of Angus, she spent most of her life in England, and her marriage to the Earl of Lennox was a key component of Henry VIII's policy of intervention in Scotland. Mistrusted by Elizabeth, she intrigued tirelessly for the marriage of her son, Darnley, to Mary. After Darnley's assassination, she initially blamed Mary, but was later persuaded of the queen's innocence.

Dudley, John, Viscount Lisle, Duke of Northumberland (c. 1504–1553) Dudley led the English army in Scotland in 1542, and persuaded Henry to cease from outright war on the kingdom after James V's death. He was appointed as a councillor for the regency of Edward VI. By late 1549, he dominated both king and council and took the title of Duke of Northumberland. In 1553, he was executed, for his part in enthroning Lady Jane Grey in England.

Dudley, Robert, Earl of Leicester (c. 1533–1588) The fifth son of the Duke of Northumberland, Robert was a companion to the young Edward VI. After Elizabeth I's accession, she seemed deeply in love with him, and his wife's mysterious death was rumoured to be murder. Mary publicly mocked the situation, saying that Elizabeth 'intended to marry her Master of the Horse, who [had] murdered his wife to make room for her'. Later, Elizabeth proposed him as a husband for Mary, who was originally insulted, but willing to consider it, in return for acknowledgement as Elizabeth's heir. Leicester disliked the idea, and wrote an apology to Mary, lest he be thought presumptuous.

Edward VI, King of England (1537–1553) The longed-for male heir of Henry VIII and his third wife, Jane Seymour, Edward became king at the age of nine. Until Mary was taken to France, the pro-English faction in Scotland wanted her to marry him. His reign ended with his early death, aged fifteen.

Elisabeth of Valois, Queen of Spain (1546–1568) Mary's sister-in-law and childhood friend, she was married to Philip II of Spain after the Treaty of Cateau-Cambrésis. Her mother, Catherine de' Medici, warned her to discourage a marriage between Mary and Elisabeth's step-son, Don Carlos. Philip was devoted to her, and their two daughters. She died in childbed, aged just 23.

Elizabeth I, Queen of England (1533–1603) Elizabeth was queen of England for forty-five years, during which time the Protestant Reformation was completed, and England began to expand its territory in the Americas. Fear of Mary's claim to the English throne dominated English politics for over twenty-five years.

Erskine, John, 6th Lord Erskine, later Earl of Mar (d. 1572) Erskine was one of the four guardians of the infant Queen Mary's person, and accompanied her to France in 1548. Although a Protestant, he tried to keep neutral in the faction fighting of Mary's reign, and she trusted him with the safety of her son, James. With that, he transferred his loyalty, and he was a strong support of the King's Party. He became regent in 1571, but died shortly afterwards – possibly poisoned by Morton, who succeeded him.

Erskine, Margaret, Lady Douglas (d. 1572) Mistress of James V, and mother of Moray, it was at Margaret's castle at Lochleven that Mary was imprisoned after Carberry Hill. Unsurprisingly, Lady Douglas did all in her power to promote her son as regent and she was not a very sympathetic gaoler for Mary.

Fleming, Mary (1542 -1600) Daughter of Lady Fleming, who was James V's half-sister, she accompanied Mary to France. On her return to the Scottish court, she was admired for her vivacity. After a long courtship, she married Mary's Secretary, Maitland of Lethington. Following his death defending Edinburgh Castle, she pleaded with the English minister, Cecil, for his body to be spared the ignominies associated with an accusation of treason.

François II, King of France (1544–1560) François inherited the French throne at the age of fifteen. Married to Mary, his short reign was dominated by her Guise relatives. He died painfully of an abscess in the ear.

Gordon, George, 4th Earl of Huntly (1513–1562) First cousin to Mary's father, James V, Huntly was the most powerful noble in north-east Scotland and acted as regent during James' absence in France.

Gordon, George, 5th Earl of Huntly (d. 1576) After the defeat of his father's rebellion at Corrigie, Lord George was imprisoned for treason. Mary later pardoned him and after he supported her during the Chaseabout Raid, restored his title and estates. Despite his conversion to Protestantism, he was appointed Chancellor. Later, he claimed that Moray and Maitland had arranged Darnley's death, and offered to prove his claim in a duel. He remained a devoted adherent of the Queen's Party and worked for Mary's restoration.

Gordon, Jean, Countess of Bothwell (c. 1546–1629) The sister of 5th Earl of Huntly, she was appointed maid-of-honour to Mary. Although Catholic, she married Bothwell in 1566 in a Protestant ceremony, and Mary provided the wedding dress. Just over a year later, she was granted a divorce on grounds of his adultery with her maid. She married the Earl of Sutherland in 1573, then, in 1594, Alexander Ogilvie.

Gordon, Sir John (d. 1562) A younger son of 4th Earl of Huntly, he fancied himself as a candidate for Mary's hand. He and his mistress, Lady Ogilvie, persuaded Lord Ogilvie that his son, James, had made advances to Lady Ogilvie, so Lord Ogilvie left his property to Sir John. When he had got everything he could from Lady Ogilvie,

Gordon imprisoned her, and he seriously wounded the new, disinherited, Lord Ogilvie in a brawl. He escaped from prison, and, when his family would not surrender him, Mary led an army north. Gordon was executed in Mary's presence, a proceeding that prostrated her with horror.

Hamilton, James, 2nd Earl of Arran, Duke of Châtelherault (c. 1519–1575) As the nearest male heir, Arran, as he then was, took up the governorship of Scotland during Mary's minority. A vacillating man, he was not widely respected and his initial pro-English, pro-Protestant policy was rejected in favour of the traditional French alliance. He was persuaded to accept Mary's marriage to the dauphin of France by the grant of a French dukedom. His support for Mary during her personal rule was patchy, but he was full-hearted in his support for her after the forced abdication, so she once again appointed him her lieutenant – a meaningless appointment, as Moray had grabbed the reigns of power.

Hamilton, John, Archbishop of St Andrews (c. 1511–1571) Half-brother of the Duke of Châtelherault, he was the last Catholic archbishop of St Andrews. Once Protestantism was established as the state religion, his role diminished, Nevertheless, he baptised Mary's son, James, and annulled the marriage of Bothwell and Lady Jean Gordon.

Hardwick, Elizabeth (Bess), Countess of Shrewsbury (c. 1527–1608) Bess' four marriages raised her from minor gentry to the richest woman in England, after the queen. Her fourth marriage was to the Earl of Shrewsbury. Once he had been given custody of Mary, the couple's life was transformed. Initially, Bess and Mary got on well, but over time, the relationship became strained. Bess accused her husband of conducting an affair with Mary, and the queen retaliated by passing on derogatory remarks Bess had apparently made about Elizabeth I. The Shrewsbury marriage collapsed in public acrimony. Bess spent much of her vast fortune on building projects – Chatsworth and Hardwick Hall in particular, and also promoting the prospects of her granddaughter, Arbella Stuart, niece to

Mary's husband, Darnley, and a contender for the English throne.

Henri II, King of France (1519–1559) Third son of François I, he spent five years of his childhood as a hostage in Spain, an experience that gave an abiding personal element to the old Franco-Spanish rivalry. Married to Catherine de' Medici, he conducted an affair with the much-older Diane de Poitiers for all his adult life. He promoted French influence in Scotland and persuaded Mary to will her crown, in default of heirs, to France. He died after a jousting accident.

Henri III, King of France (1551–1589) Fourth son of Henri II and Catherine de' Medici, he was Duke of Anjou, before being elected to the throne of Poland. Once King of France, he attempted to pursue a path of religious tolerance, but was assassinated by a Catholic fanatic.

Henry VIII, King of England (1491–1547) Henry began his reign in traditional fashion, promoting war with Scotland's ally, France. and expressing strong support for papal authority. By the late 1520s however, a combination of dynastic fears and his passion for Anne Boleyn, led him to request Pope Clement VII to grant an annulment of his marriage to Katharine of Aragon. When it was not forthcoming, he broke with Rome, took the title Supreme Head of the Church in England and pursued a policy of ruthless repression of all dissent. Throughout his reign, he interfered in Scottish domestic politics, determined to prove that he was the overlord of the Scottish monarchs.

Hepburn, James, Earl of Bothwell (c. 1534–1578) Despite early conversion to Protestantism, Bothwell supported Marie of Guise, and was one of the very few who took no bribes from either France or Scotland. On Mary's return, he was loyal, but frequently involved in disputes with others, particularly Moray. Mary relied on him heavily, although there is no evidence of any relationship before Darnley's death. Whether Bothwell was the prime mover or the scapegoat for Darnley's assassination is disputed. Similarly, whether he abducted and raped Mary against her will,

or whether they colluded is also argued. She married him, gave him the title of Duke of Orkney and refused to give him up to the Lords. He went into exile in Denmark, and died in prison there, having lost his sanity.

Howard, Thomas, 4th Duke of Norfolk (1536–1572) Thomas inherited the dukedom of Norfolk from his grandfather. He was Elizabeth I's proxy for the signing of the Treaty of Berwick. In the late 1560s, a marriage between Norfolk and Mary was mooted. Whilst it had widespread support amongst Elizabeth I's councillors, she was furious when she discovered the plan, and Norfolk was imprisoned. Released, he became entangled in the Ridolfi Plot and was executed for treason.

James IV, King of Scots (1473–1513) James, an intelligent and capable king, led a resurgence in Scottish influence and military strength, but was killed at the Battle of Flodden.

James V, King of Scots (1512–1542) James sought to impose his authority after a troubled minority, during which his uncle, Henry VIII of England, attempted to destabilise his government. James, having made huge progress, died aged thirty. He was a great Renaissance prince – enhancing Scottish castles in French-Renaissance style.

James VI & I, King of Scots, King of England (1566–1625) Son of Mary and Darnley, James became King of Scots at just over a year old when her lords forced his mother to abdicate. He became the first monarch to rule throughout the British Isles in March 1603. HM Queen Elizabeth II is his direct descendant.

Melville, Sir James, of Halhill (c. 1535–1617) Although a Protestant, and an associate of Moray, Melville was loyal personally to Mary, and acted as her envoy to deliver to Elizabeth I the news of the birth of James. Avoiding factional politics, he hoped to reconcile Mary to the lords after her enforced abdication, but failed. He served all four of James' regents, and Mary remembered him fondly enough to recommend him to James.

His memoirs are an important source for the period.

Killigrew, Sir Henry (c. 1525–1603) An ardent Protestant, Killigrew served Elizabeth I as ambassador and diplomat, doing everything he could to undermine Catholicism at home and abroad. He was Cecil's brother-in-law, and, like him, distrusted Mary. He was given the mission of persuading the acting Scottish government to receive Mary back into the country, and dispatch her, to avoid Elizabeth having to take open action.

Kirkcaldy, Sir William, of Grange (c. 1520 -1573) An early Protestant, he was amongst the assassins of Cardinal Beaton besieged at St Andrew's. He fought with the Lords of the Congregation and favoured an English alliance. He was with Moray in the Chaseabout Raid but was later pardoned. An enemy of Bothwell's, he accused him of Darnley's murder, and wrote to his English friend, Bedford, that, to retain noble support, Mary must rid herself of Bothwell. Over time, he withdrew his support for the King's Party, as too dominated by England. He held Edinburgh Castle against the Regent Lennox and was executed for treason.

Knightley, Sir Richard (1533–1615) As MP for the county where Fotheringhay was situated, he witnessed Mary's execution.

Knox, John (c. 1514–1576) One of the most influential Scotsmen who has ever lived, Knox was ordained priest in the late 1530s. He was converted to Protestantism by George Wishart, and began a career of preaching and writing that brought him into conflict with the government. Exiled, he strongly influenced the English Protestants of Edward VI's reign. Returning to Scotland, he worked with the Lords of the Congregation against Marie of Guise, and when Mary returned, he was bitterly hostile to her, personally and politically. A close ally of Moray, he preached his funeral sermon. His *Book of Discipline* was fundamental to Protestantism in Scotland.

Leslie, John, Bishop of Ross (1527–1596) The bishop was a dedicated supporter of Mary's from 1560, and was entrusted by the queen with her will and jewels when she was in childbirth. During Mary's exile, he acted as her agent and was instrumental in the plan for her to marry Norfolk. Allegedly, while being questioned in the Tower of London, he accused Mary of the murder of Darnley. Eventually released, he spent the rest of his life trying to promote the Catholic faith in Scotland. He wrote the *History of Scotland,* an account sympathetic to Mary.

Lindsay, David, 10th Earl of Crawford (c. 1526–1574) Crawford was a consistent supporter of Mary. He was cupbearer at her wedding to Darnley and rode with her in the Chaseabout Raid. After her escape from Lochleven, he joined the association for her defence, but, like Huntly, arrived too late to change the outcome of the Battle of Langside.

Lindsay, Patrick, 6th Lord Lindsay of the Byres (c. 1521–1589) An early, committed Protestant, he objected vociferously to Mary hearing Mass. Later, he seemed on better terms with her and, on one occasion at least, partnered her in an archery competition. Married to Euphemia Douglas of Lochleven, Moray's half-sister, it was Lindsay who compelled Mary to abdicate by threatening her with violence.

Livingston, Alexander, 5th Lord (d. c. 1553) Livingston was one of the four nobles appointed as guardians of the infant Queen Mary's person. His son, the 6th Lord, despite being a Protestant, was one of Mary's staunchest supporters, and his daughter, Mary Livingston, one of her band of friends.

Livingston, Mary (c. 1541–1585) One of the queen's Four Marys, she accompanied Mary to France and was a leading light of the Scottish court. Mary provided her dowry and a magnificent wedding. She accompanied Mary to Lochleven, but not into exile. Her eldest son became ambassador from James VI to Elizabeth I.

Maitland, Sir William, of Lethington (d. 1573) Although at least nominally Protestant, Maitland did not appear driven by the sectarianism of the time and was appointed Secretary to Marie of Guise, a role he used to spy for the Lords of the Congregation and their English allies. He defected to the Lords in October 1559. He was appointed Mary's Secretary on her return, but was exiled after involvement in Riccio's murder. Reinstated, his loyalty faltered after her marriage to Bothwell. He was a prominent member of the King's Party initially, but ultimately his affection for Mary and approval of her tolerant religious policy moved him to seek her reinstatement. After he was obliged to surrender Edinburgh Castle, he died awaiting trial for treason, possibly by his own hand.

Marie of Guise, Queen-consort and Regent of Scotland (1516–1560) Niece of the Duke of Lorraine, Marie married the Duke of Longueville, by whom she had two sons. On his death, she was mooted as a wife for Henry VIII of England, but was eventually married to James V. She had two sons, who both died as infants, before Mary. Throughout Mary's childhood, Marie's chief aim was to maintain her daughter's crown and the Franco-Scots alliance.

Mary I, Queen of England (1516–1558) Daughter of Henry VIII and his first wife, Katharine of Aragon, Mary became England's first Queen-regnant in 1553. She sought to reinstate Catholicism following the brief reign of her Protestant half-brother, Edward VI, but died after a reign of only five years, to be succeeded by her Protestant half-sister, Elizabeth I.

Paulet, Sir Amyas (c. 1532–1588) Paulet was governor of Jersey for many years and then served as English ambassador to France, where, as a Puritan, he sympathised strongly with the Huguenot cause. He was appointed Mary's gaoler in April 1585 and continued in that role until her execution. He was an unsympathetic and harsh gaoler. He pushed Elizabeth I to have the death sentence carried out, but absolutely refused Elizabeth's request to secretly murder Mary.

Philip II, King of Spain, Duke of Burgundy (1527–1598) Philip inherited Spain as well as the Netherlands from his father, Emperor Charles V. Whilst he eventually brought the Italian Wars to an end with the Treaty of Cateau-Cambrésis, much of his life was devoted to protecting Catholicism in Europe and trying to maintain control of the Netherlands. Mary bequeathed him her claim to the English throne.

Poitiers, Diane de (1499–1566) Diane was a French noblewomen who served several queens of France before becoming the long-term mistress of Henri II. During his reign, she wielded considerable political influence and was well known to Mary during her youth.

Pius V, (Giovanni Angelo de' Medici) (1499–1565) Elected in 1559, he convened the final session of the Council of Trent and confirmed its findings in the bull *Benedictus Deus*. He encouraged Mary to reinstitute Catholicism in Scotland, but she was reluctant to overturn the Protestant settlement.

Randolph, Sir Thomas (1525–1590) He travelled extensively in France and came to the notice of the English ambassador there, who secured him a seat in the English Parliament. He also built a relationship with Scottish Protestants there and after Mary's return had an unofficial diplomatic role for England at the Scottish court, where he became enamoured of Mary Beaton. In 1566, he was expelled for involvement in a plot against Mary. Subsequently, Elizabeth I posted him to Russia.

Riccio, David (1533–1566) He entered Mary's employ as a musician, then became her French secretary and confidant. Suspected of taking bribes and of influencing Mary unduly, he became the focus of resentment. Darnley's jealousy was whipped up, and he, along with Morton and others broke into Mary's apartments, dragged Riccio out and stabbed him to death.

Ridolfi, Roberto di (1531–1612) Ridolfi, a Florentine banker in London, acted as go-between for Mary, the Bishop of Ross, the Pope, Philip II of Spain, the Duke of Norfolk and others, as a plot was conceived to free Mary and put her on the English throne. It appears that Ridolfi was a double agent – acting for Walsingham as well. Where his true loyalties lay cannot be ascertained. In France when the plans came to light, he remained in Europe for the rest of his life.

Ronsard, Pierre de (1524–1585) He spent a year of his youth at the court of James V, before returning to France where he became one of the most feted court poets. He wrote poetry in praise of Mary's beauty.

Russell, Francis, 2nd Earl of Bedford (1527–1585) A confirmed Protestant, he was an English Privy Councillor from the start of Elizabeth I's reign. She sent him to France on the death of François to obtain Mary's signature to the Treaty of Edinburgh. Appointed Warden of the East Marches and Governor of Berwick, he played a major part in Anglo-Scots diplomacy until 1567, when he failed to gain Elizabeth I's open support for the Scots rebels.

Ruthven, Patrick, 4th Earl of Ruthven (1520–1566) Provost of Perth for many years, he refused Marie of Guise's command that Catholic worship be enforced in the town, provoking her to take the town with French-paid troops. He mediated between Marie and the Lords of the Congregation, although his sympathies were with the lords. He joined Mary's Council, although she and Moray both disliked him personally. Despite debilitating illness, he was one of the chief assassins of Riccio, and fled into England, where he died within months.

Sadler, Sir Ralph (1507–1587) A servant of the English minister, Thomas Cromwell, he survived his master's downfall and was sent by Henry VIII as envoy to Scotland in the wake of James V's death, but he struggled to master Scottish politics. Later, he served in Somerset's wars against Scotland. He was appointed Mary's gaoler in 1584 and treated her gently, but later argued forcefully for her execution.

Seton, Mary (c. 1541–after 1615) Daughter of 4th Lord Seton, she accompanied Mary to France and returned with her in 1561. Seton disguised herself as the queen to enable Mary to escaple from Lochleven. She remained with Mary, rejecting all offers of marriage,

and accompanied her into exile in England. She was famed for her ability to dress Mary's beautiful hair. By 1583, poor health led her to ask for release from the queen's service. She retired to the convent of St-Pierre-aux-Dames, where Mary's aunt was abbess, and died there some thirty-five years later.

Seymour, Edward, Duke of Somerset (c. 1500–1552) Brother-in-law of Henry VIII of England, he was a leading councillor to that king and a military commander of high repute, leading the English forces against Scotland. On Henry's death, he took on the role of Lord Protector, and prosecuted the war against Scotland viciously.

Spens, John, of Condie, Queen's Advocate (d. 1573) By 1539, Spens was one of the nine leading Edinburgh lawyers permitted to argue all matters before the College of Justice. Appointed as advocate to Marie of Guise, he negotiated with the Lords of the Congregation. He retained the office under Mary, and was also a Councillor and important member of the Edinburgh Town Council. He avoided taking any part in the tumults of the reign.

Stewart, James, Earl of Moray (1531–1570) An illegitimate son of James V, he accompanied Mary to France in 1548, but then returned. He was on good terms with his stepmother, Marie of Guise, until he converted to Protestantism. He was reluctant to openly rebel, but eventually joined the Lords of the Congregation and promoted alliance with England. He negotiated Mary's return and was her right-hand-man until she married Darnley against his advice and he rebelled. Unaware of his involvement in Riccio's murder, Mary welcomed him home after it. He took great care to be absent from the scene at the time of Darnley's death, but it is extremely likely he knew of the plans, and may have been more heavily involved. He took the regency on Mary's abdication, and did everything he could to vilify her with Elizabeth I. Nevertheless, he faced significant unrest, and Mary's supporters continued the fight. Chief amongst the Queen's Party were the Hamiltons, and it was a member of this clan, James Hamilton of Bothwellhaugh, who assassinated Moray.

Stewart, Jean, Countess of Argyll (d. 1588)
Mary's illegitimate half-sister, and was present when Riccio was murdered. She had an unhappy marriage, which Mary tried to patch up, but a divorce was granted in 1573. Jean was proxy for Elizabeth I at the christening of Prince James, an action for which John Knox publicly rebuked her.

Stuart, Lady Arbella (1575–1615) Arbella's father was Lord Charles Stuart, Darnley's younger brother. Orphaned as an infant she was taken into the household of her maternal grandmother, Lady Shrewsbury, where Mary was imprisoned. Mary was fond of her niece, and tried to ensure she inherited the earldom of Lennox. Later, Arbella's secret marriage ended with imprisonment and death after she refused to eat.

Stuart, Henry, Lord Darnley, King of Scots (1545–1567) Great-grandson of Henry VII, and son of the Earl of Lennox, he had a claim to both the English and Scottish thrones. He first met Mary in France in 1560, then visited her in 1565 when Elizabeth I suggested him as a possible husband. Elizabeth changed her mind, and recalled him, but Mary had determined to marry him. On paper, the match was excellent, but his many character flaws and eagerness for power resulted in the marriage breaking down within months. He was equally unpopular with the Scottish nobles. Who orchestrated his assassination has been debated since the day it occurred.

Stuart, Matthew, 4th Earl of Lennox (1516–1571) A Scots nobleman, married to the half-sister of James V, he was Mary's father-in-law. He brought a private prosecution against Bothwell for the assassination of Darnley. He became regent for Mary's son but was assassinated during the struggle for control between the Queen's Party and the King's Party.

Talbot, George, 6th Earl of Shrewsbury (c. 1522–1590) Shrewsbury had an impressive early career, and by 1565 was joint Lieutenant-General of the North. He married Elizabeth Hardwick as her fourth husband. Their happy domestic life was turned upside down when Elizabeth I appointed Shrewsbury as Mary's 'guardian'. The stress and expense of this role ruined his marriage, his finances and his health. Although he carried out his duties faithfully, long acquaintanceship with Mary led him to request Elizabeth I to excuse his presence at Mary's execution. His plea was refused.

Throckmorton, Sir Nicholas (1516–1571) Throckmorton had a moderately successful career as an English MP and diplomat, and was sent by Elizabeth I to try to improve Mary's lot when she was at Lochleven, to little avail.

Walsingham, Sir Francis (c 1532–1590) Walsingham, a firm Protestant, was Elizabeth I's ambassador to France where he witnessed the Massacre of St Bartholomew. This convinced him England was vulnerable to Catholic plotting and that Mary was an enemy of the English state. His patient work led to the uncovering of the Babington Plot – although he probably had a hand in inciting it.

INDEX OF EVENTS

A short description of events that are not self-explanatory.

January

- In the late 1550s, Scotland headed for civil war as the Protestant Lords of the Congregation sought to distance the country from its old alliance with France and its adherence to the Catholic faith, both represented by Marie of Guise, regent for her daughter, Queen Mary. The Lords sought help from Protestant England.

- The Earl of Morton was one of the chief conspirators in the murder of Riccio, despite being Mary's Chancellor. After Mary regained control of events, Morton was banished and went to England. He was forgiven and allowed to return.

- The Reformation Parliament outlawed the Catholic Mass and implemented Protestantism. The authority of the pope was rejected, and the Treaty of Berwick with England was ratified.

- On arrival in England, Mary saw herself as a guest, but as the York Commission proceeded, it became apparent that she would not be permitted to leave. She was moved further away from the Anglo-Scots border to prevent any rescue attempt, and taken to Tutbury Castle.

- The Westminster Commission succeeded that of York, which had been called in the autumn of 1568 to determine the guilt or innocence of Mary, with regard to the assassination of Darnley. Mary rejected its authority. Moray attended in person, and the infamous Casket Letters were produced.

- In 1569 the Duke of Norfolk agreed a plan to marry Mary. Elizabeth I's other ministers approved, but Elizabeth herself was not informed, and when she discovered it she was furious. Norfolk managed to avoid serious punishment but later became embroiled in the Ridolfi Plot to free Mary, for which he was executed.

- Although Mary and Darnley had been reconciled following the murder of Riccio, once Prince James was christened, Mary avoided her husband as much as possible. In January 1567, she sought a rapprochement and he returned to Edinburgh.

- The final death sentence against Mary was passed by the English Parliament. After that, her confinement became even more strict and her personal servants were replaced with English government appointees.

- The earldom of Moray had been administered by the Earl of Huntly since 1549. Lord James Stewart requested that Mary give it to him, and this grant was an inciting factor in Huntly's rebellion.

February

- The plot to assassinate Mary's secretary, David Riccio, was well known in both Scotland and England. Mary dismissed the warning she received from James Melville with the comment that 'our countrymen are well-wordy'.

- Within days of Darnley's assassination the finger of suspicion was pointed at the Earl of Bothwell, and shortly thereafter at Mary herself. Anonymous placards appeared around Edinburgh accusing Bothwell and Mary of adultery and murder.

- In 1565, Matthew Stuart, Earl of Lennox, and his son, Lord Darnley, who were both denizens of England, were granted permission to go to Scotland to reclaim Lennox lands. When Lennox and Darnley refused to obey Elizabeth I's demand that they return, Lady Lennox was sent to the Tower of London, where she remained until after Darnley's assassination.

- The Pacification of Perth was a peace settlement brokered by the English envoy, Henry Killigrew. The King's Party (supporters of the young James VI) and the Queen's Party (who wanted Mary restored), agreed to end hostilities. James was recognised as king, with Morton as regent. This ended Mary's hope of being reinstated as sovereign.

- In a letter written in a more straightforward style than Elizabeth I was wont to use, she urged Mary to seek out and punish those responsible for Darnley's murder, no matter how close they were to the queen.

- The Treaty of Berwick, signed by the Duke of Norfolk for Elizabeth I, and by the Duke of Châtelherault for Scotland, agreed that an English army and fleet would be sent to Scotland to help the Lords of the Congregation to oust Marie of Guise from the regency, and remove French troops from Scotland.

March

- Opposition to Mary focused on her secretary, David Riccio, whom her lords believed to be influencing her against them. A bond was drawn up by the consiprators to force Mary to grant Darnley the Crown Matrimonial, reinstate the rebels and confirm Protestantism. No mention was made of the assassination of Riccio, but that was the hidden aim, with Darnley to be involved.

- Mary was eager to be named as heir to the English crown. Elizabeth I did not want to confirm that, for various reasons, including fear of assassination. Elizabeth intimated that, if Mary married her nominee, Leicester, the succession would be secured to her.

- After Riccio's murder, Mary persuaded Darnley that he had been duped, and the pair escaped from Edinburgh to Dunbar. Mary called on her loyal subjects to attend her armed, and she soon returned to the capital. The assassins were banished, except Moray, as Mary did not know of his involvement.

- In the wake of Darnley's death, Mary was slow to act against his assassins, for reasons that are unclear. Eventually, her father-in-law, who was the only one interested in avenging Darnley, was permitted to bring a private prosecution against the man rumoured to be the ringleader – James Hepburn, Earl of Bothwell.

April

- According to the marriage treaty of Mary and François, any son would inherit both kingdoms, if they had only daughters, the eldest would inherit the Scottish Crown, and if they had no children, the Scottish Crown would revert to Mary's next heirs, the Hamiltons. Before her marriage, the sixteen-year-old queen was persuaded to sign an agreement that, should she die childless, her kingdom would pass to the French Crown.

- In April, returning to Edinburgh from a visit to Prince James at Stirling, Mary and her escort were stopped by the Earl of Bothwell. Unable to resist his superior force, or, some believe, having made a previous agreement with him, Mary was taken by him to Dunbar Castle. There, he either forced her to accept him as her husband, by raping her, or persuaded her that it was the solution to her problems and would have the support of her lords.

- Lennox brought a private prosecution, and, fearing for his own safety, came to Edinburgh with a large force. Lennox was informed he could only take in an escort of a dozen men, so, with Bothwell heavily armed, Lennox was, in effect, prevented from attending the trial and running the prosecution. With no evidence brought against him, Bothwell was acquitted.

- After Darnley's death, Mary leant on Bothwell for advice. He persuaded twenty-four of her nobles to sign a bond, recommending that she marry him. According to Mary, it was this document that persuaded her to accept Bothwell as her husband, after he abducted her. Most of the signatories later condemned the marriage.

May

- During the late 1550s, the nascent Kirk was diverging from the Catholic Church, and the new doctrines being preached by dedicated men throughout the land. Four preachers were summoned to appear at Sterling on 10th May 1559 and, as they travelled, they drew a crowd of supporters.

- Defeated at Langside, Mary had three choices – to retreat to the Highlands and gather support from the earls of Huntly and Argyll; take ship for France, or cross the Solway Firth into England and request help from Elizabeth I of England. Against advice, she decided on the latter course, which proved the worst mistake of her life.

- From the moment of her return to Scotland in 1561, Mary vigorously promoted the idea of a personal meeting between herself and Elizabeth I of England. Elizabeth was reluctant to agree, until Mary signed the Treaty of Edinburgh, confirming Elizabeth as rightful queen of England. Eventually, the decision was made that they should meet at York in 1562. Cecil did everything he could to block the meeting, and the massacre of Huguenots by Mary's uncle, the Duke of Guise, played into his hands. The meeting was postponed indefinitely.

June

- Following the loss of the Battle of Solway Moss, in 1542, a number of Scots nobles were captured by the English. They were taken to the court of Henry VIII, and promised freedom and pensions, if they swore an oath to Henry, promising to promote English interests in Scotland, against the traditional Franco-Scots alliance. This was to include marriage between Mary, and Henry's son, later Edward VI.

- Although Mary and Bothwell appeared to have survived their marriage politically intact, before long there was open rebellion.

- After the inconoclastic attacks on Perth, the town was surrounded by Marie of Guise's troops. This was considered a breaking of her oath, as she had sworn she would not pay Scotsmen to fight against Scotsmen. The regent believed she had avoided breaking her word by paying the troops with French gold.

July

- James Hamilton, Earl of Arran, was instituted as Governor of the Realm, and Tutor to the infant Mary, after James V's death. He sympathised with Protestantism and advocated compromise with England. The Treaty of Greenwich provided for a cessation of the war,

with Mary to marry Prince Edward, and be taken to England for her upbringing.

- During her captivity, the once-athletic Mary suffered declining health. The pains in her side, which she had experienced all her life, continued, along with rheumatism, and increasing weight from lack of exercise. By summer 1586 her legs were swollen and inflamed.

- In 1585-6, Elizabeth I knew that war with Spain was inevitable. She needed to protect the Anglo-Scottish border, so entered into negotiations with James VI, whom she had previously refused to recognise as King of Scots. He was also excepted from the English Parliamentary act that automatically excluded from the throne anyone who benefited from the assassination of Elizabeth, even if they were innocent of the deed. A new Treaty of Berwick recognised James as king and gave him a hefty subsidy. James' signature effectively ended his mother's hopes of freedom and of life. Mary was now expendable.

- The 1543 Treaty of Greenwich agreed by Arran was rejected by Parliament. Instead, the Franco-Scottish alliance was revived. The French sent troops and money to ward off the English, and, in the Treaty of Haddington, agreed a match between the French dauphin and Mary.

- As 1586 unfolded, Walsingham laid a snare to catch Mary. He infiltrated, perhaps even incited, a plot by Anthony Babington and others to assassinate Elizabeth I and free Mary. Well aware of every turn of events, he could safely inform Leicester that the net was closing on Mary.

- In 1563, following an accusation that he had incited the Earl of Arran to kidnap Mary, Bothwell was imprisoned. He escaped, and was captured by the English en route to France. Released from the Tower of London after Mary's intervention, he went to France, armed with a recommendation from the queen for a military position. He returned briefly to Scotland, was outlawed again, then summoned home by Mary who needed support for her marriage to Darnley.

- After her surrender at Carberry Hill, Mary was imprisoned at Lochleven in harsh circumstances. Whilst there, she suffered a miscarriage. She was bullied and humiliated, and, threatened by Lord Lindsay of the Byres that he would cut her throat if she did not submit, signed a document of abdication. She later held it to be invalid as obtained under duress.

August

- When Mary first contemplated returning to Scotland in 1561, it was suggested that she land in the territories of the 4th Earl of Huntly and reinstate Catholicism in Scotland, a plan she rejected. Huntly's rivalry with Mary's half-brother, Lord James Stewart was exacerbated by Mary's grant to the latter of the earldom of Moray. Moray persuaded Mary that Huntly had to be tamed, and together they led an army north to defeat the Gordon clan at the Battle of Corrigie.

- When Mary returned to Scotland in 1561, it was agreed that she would worship as a Catholic in the privacy of her own chapel. More stringent Protestants objected to this, and were vigilant to ensure that the agreement was strictly adhered to. Any celebration of Mass without the queen's presence attracted anger and violence.

- The exact timing and location of Mary's arrival in France is not certain. It seems most likely that an original landing was made at Roscoff, and then the party travelled on by sea to St-Pol-de-Lèon.

- Whilst Mary had accepted the 1560 Acts instituting Protestantism as Scotland's state religion, she did not formally ratify them. This probably underlay the constant suspicion that she intended to restore Catholicism, although there is no other evidence to support such an intention.

- Exiled from Scotland, Knox was also unwelcome in England, as Elizabeth I was angered by his book *The First Blast of the Trumpet against the Monstrous Regiment of Women*, which attacked the legitimacy of female rule.

September

- Moray was succeeded as regent by the Earl of Lennox, Darnley's father, who was the nominee of Elizabeth I. He too, was killed, perhaps as an act of assassination, in an affray with the Queen's Party.

- In 1571, after the failure of the Rising of the North to free Mary and place her on the English throne, Mary began a secret correspondence with Spain. A Florentine banker, Roberto di Ridolfi, acted as intermediary between Mary; her agent, the Bishop of Ross; the Duke of Norfolk and others. It's possible Ridolfi was in the pay of Walsingham. Discovery of the correspondence led to Norfolk's execution for treason.

- Elizabeth I claimed she could not help Mary regain her throne until the latter's innocence of the murder of Darnley was established. A hearing was begun at York, which Moray attended, bringing a series of letters, allegedly found in a casket belonging to Mary. These letters had not previously been circulated, but were now found to contain enough material to make Mary appear guilt of adultery and murder. Mary denied their authorship, pointing out that her writing was easy to forge. The authenticity of the letters has been debated ever since, especially as the originals were lost or deliberately destroyed in the 1580s.

- In September 1559, a Scots delegation came to France to finalise the marriage treaty. Nine of them, including Lord James Stewart, fell ill on the return journey, and five died. Although Knox hinted darkly of poisoning by Mary's Guise family, it was probably a simple case of food-poisoning.

- During Mary's infancy, the earls of Lennox and Arran had been rivals for power. Lennox lost the battle, and was exiled to England, where he swore allegiance to Henry VIII, and married Henry's niece, Lady Margaret Douglas, son of the Earl of Angus, who had already taken Henry's shilling. On Mary's return, Lennox and Lady Lennox, who was Mary's aunt, petitioned for restoration of the Lennox lands.

- In 1550, Marie of Guise visited to France, where she was reunited with her daughter, and her son from her first marriage. She stayed several months, renewing her friendship with Henri II who continued to support her in Scotland. She returned home via England, where she was feted at the English court.

- Although Mary had appeared to be reconciled with Darnley to the extent that he acknowledged their son as his own, contradicting ugly rumours that James was Riccio's son, once this had been done Mary treated her husband with barely-disguised contempt. He did little to earn any better opinion.

October

- Following the execution of Babington, Mary was tried for treason under the English Act of Association. Thirty-six commissioners were appointed, including her former gaoler, the Earl of Shrewsbury, Cecil and Walsingham. Mary was not permitted legal counsel, and no witnesses for the prosecution were brought forward for her to question.

- When Elizabeth I fell ill with small-pox, her councillors were divided as to who should succeed her. Dudley favoured Mary, who was the heir under common law, whilst Cecil preferred Lady Katherine Grey, heir under Henry VIII's will. Other possibilities were Lady Lennox, and the Earl of Huntingdon.

- The Crown Matrimonial would have entitled Darnley to remain King of Scots, in the event of Mary's death, until his own decease, rather than the throne passing immediately to her heir. This arrangement had been agreed for François, but Mary would not countenance it for Darnley.

- Mary's visit to Bothwell during her justice-in-ayre in the Lowlands has been taken as evidence of her being in love with him, as it was a sixty-mile round trip. In fact, Mary delayed the visit for some days, the whole of her court accompanied her, and the distance was not unusually long.

- Following the trial at Fotheringhay, in accordance with Elizabeth I's orders, no sentence was given in Mary's presence. Instead, the Commissioners returned to London, and pronounced the sentence there.

November

- Sir Amyas Paulet had been a harsh and unsympathetic gaoler to Mary, delighting in petty acts of tyranny. Once the Commission had pronounced sentence in London, he came to her apartments at Fotheringhay to inform her, and to browbeat her into confessing her guilt. Mary refused to do so, and the two argued over Elizabeth I's title of 'Supreme Governor of the Church in England'.

- In the early 1580s, Mary hoped that her son would make an agreement with England that would enable her to return to Scotland as joint ruler. After negotiations in which she was, once again, betrayed, she was prepared to agree to any terms, including renouncing both crowns, in return for freedom. She was even willing to remain in England, provided she could live quietly on an income equal to that of her dower from France. James however, had let it be known to Elizabeth that Mary's freedom was not a prerequisite for a treaty between the countries.

- In 1557, the Lords of the Congregation invited Knox to return to Scotland, but then withdrew the invitation, fearing he would make a sensitive political situation worse. Knox took this as an affront to God as well as himself.

December

- In the autumn of 1566, Mary had been seriously ill, and was thought close to death when she lay in a coma. Eventually, she recovered, but was still frail until she finally vomited blood – indicating a perforated ulcer might have been the cause of her symptoms.

- Having first refused to countenance the York Commission, Mary had eventually sent representatives, believing that her innocence would be proven, and Elizabeth I would then help her regain the throne. However, when the Commission was moved to London, and Moray was allowed to appear, but Mary was not, she realised that there had never been any intention of justice being done, and recalled her representatives.

Mary, Queen of Scots Book of Days
Published in Great Britain in 2021 by
Graffeg Limited.

Written by Tudor Times
Designed and produced by Graffeg Limited
copyright © 2021

Tudor Times Ltd www.tudortimes.co.uk

Graffeg Limited, 24 Stradey Park Business
Centre, Mwrwg Road, Llangennech,
Llanelli, Carmarthenshire, SA14 8YP,
Wales, UK. Tel: 01554 824000.
www.graffeg.com.

ISBN 9781913134891

1 2 3 4 5 6 7 8 9

Photo credits:

Cover image amd page 6: Mary, Queen
of Scots (1542-87) circa 1558 by François
Clouet (c. 1520-1572), Royal Collection
Trust.

Page 5: Alamy.